PARTICLES

BOOKS BY DAN GERBER

POETRY

Particles: New and Selected Poems
Sailing through Cassiopeia
A Primer on Parallel Lives
Trying to Catch the Horses
A Last Bridge Home: New and Selected Poems
Snow on the Backs of Animals
The Chinese Poems
Departure
The Revenant

NOVELS

A Voice from the River
Out of Control
American Atlas

SHORT STORIES

Grass Fires

NONFICTION

A Second Life: A Collected Nonfiction
Indy: The World's Fastest Carnival Ride

DAN GERBER

Particles

New and Selected Poems

Copper Canyon Press
Port Townsend, Washington

Cover art: Detail of Jai Prakash Yantra, one of nineteen architectural astronomical instruments at the Jantar Mantar monument in Jaipur, Rajasthan, India.

Copper Canyon Press is in residence at Fort Worden State Park in Port Townsend, Washington, under the auspices of Centrum. Centrum is a gathering place for artists and creative thinkers from around the world, students of all ages and backgrounds, and audiences seeking extraordinary cultural enrichment.

LIBRARY OF CONGRESS CATALOGING-IN-PUBLICATION DATA

Names: Gerber, Dan, 1940– author.
Title: Particles / Dan Gerber.
Description: Port Townsend, Washington : Copper Canyon Press, 2017.
Identifiers: LCCN 2017014456 | ISBN 9781556595257 (paperback)
Subjects: | BISAC: POETRY / American / General.
Classification: LCC PS3557.E66 A6 2017 | DDC 811/.54— dc23
LC record available at https://lccn.loc.gov/2017014456

9 8 7 6 5 4 3 2 FIRST PRINTING

COPPER CANYON PRESS
Post Office Box 271
Port Townsend, Washington 98368
www.coppercanyonpress.org

ACKNOWLEDGMENTS

I wish to thank all the dedicated and talented people at Copper Canyon Press, most particularly, Joseph Bednarik for his time and good counsel, Tonaya Craft and David Caligiuri, for their great care and attention to getting everything right, George Knotek for his work raising the funds to make this book possible, Valerie Brewster, for making the book itself a thing of beauty, and most importantly, my editor, Michael Wiegers, for his dedication in helping me get the best poems in the best order and for making me make sure each one of them is the best it can be. I would like to thank Jim Harrison for fifty years of friendship, advice, and the exchange of second and third drafts, Barry Spacks, Ted Kooser, Judith Minty, and Robert VanderMolen for their long friendship and their attention to many of these poems, and George Oppen for his example, his kindness, and his encouragement so many years ago. Thanks also to Jerry Reddan of Tangram Press, who published many of these poems as visually striking broadsides, and to the editors of the print and online magazines and anthologies in which some of the new poems in this volume originally appeared, including: *American Life in Poetry, Askew, The Café Review, Caliban, Michigan Quarterly Review, Narrative, Poetry East, Rattle, Spectrum, Talking River,* and *The Writer's Almanac* (Garrison Keillor).

I would like to thank the following presses and their editors, who supported the publication of the books from which are reprinted sections of this collection:

Sumac Press: *The Revenant, Departure,* and *The Chinese Poems*
Winn Press: *Snow on the Backs of Animals*
Clark City Press: *A Last Bridge Home*

Poems from *Trying to Catch the Horses* are republished with permission of Michigan State University Press, from *Trying to Catch the Horses* by Dan Gerber, copyright 1999; permission conveyed through Copyright Clearance Center, Inc.

To Deb, always

And, in memoriam, to
Jim Harrison
Kobun Chino, Sensei
Bob Watkins
and
Barry Spacks

To study the way is to study the self.
To study the self is to forget the self.
To forget the self is to be awakened to all things.

DŌGEN, AD 1233

I was the world in which I walked, and what I saw
Or heard or felt came not but from myself;
And there I found myself more truly and more strange.

WALLACE STEVENS, 1921

First Light

Morning, busy in the distance,
hammer blows, airplane in clouds.

Crows, muffled growling of a saw, steady pulse
of silence holding it together.

Pause between breathing in,
and out.

Thought of air thinking
day's first light.

Foothills flaunting their ridges.

Losing the moment as I saw it;
finding it in its changes.

Contents

from **A LAST BRIDGE HOME** (1992)

from **TRYING TO CATCH THE HORSES** (1999)

from **A PRIMER ON PARALLEL LIVES** (2007)

NEW POEMS

PARTICLES

Particles

The reason you do not clearly understand
the time-being
is that you think of time only as passing.

DŌGEN, AD 1240

We must endure our thoughts all night, until
The bright obvious stands motionless in cold.

WALLACE STEVENS, 1946

Winter solstice—the sun
stopped for a moment—
can you feel its light stretching—
as it shrugs off its migration
and turns back north toward the pole?

■ ■ ■

On this rock, just the right
distance from the nearest star,
sheltered by Jupiter and kept in season
by the steadying moon,
being moves through my body
like clouds, arriving in one shape,
drifting off as another.

I don't remember being born,
only the great dog
whose fur I clung to
before the first day of school.

Memory accounts
for space, not time.

It records the quality and angle
of light, the keen, metallic scent of wind
through porch screens—the wailing
as it rises—the warmth and texture of air—
the weather and sometimes
whether or not it was a Tuesday,
but never how long it lasted—or
how many years ago—only
how it felt—alone in that moment.
And the sound of waves breaking.

We see time past as Euclidian—moments
of solitude with no date affixed—
long afternoons of childhood in no time at all,
when it first occurred that you were seven,
without knowing that,
because of the moment—now in memory—
you will always be seven in that place.

Our solitude—being alone
with the one you knew there—
our loneliness—being there
without him.

Two billion seconds of life
now, on a planet only
four and a half billion years
old—and every atom on loan
to it much older than that.

■ ■ ■

In the beginning, all that was
was too hot for atoms — too tightly
packed to let go of its light —
as if the universe
had come out the other side of a black hole —
heading back to where it began
over ungraspable distance
right now — and not at all
far from home.

Every creation story I know
comes out of the dark —
the brune garden in which light blooms.
Dark matter pulling chaotic
energy apart — breaking the prison
of its own concentration —

giving it space to be a wave.

■ ■ ■

The master equation
of the Standard Model of particle physics
accounts for everything
except gravity — and gravity
accounts for everything —
irresistible center of the spheres
and stars, on and among which
we go on — curving our
straight course — as it draws
the low-gliding hawk
irresistibly
back together with its shadow.

Imagine Earth
as the nucleus of a hydrogen atom
from which we're looking out—hoping
for a glimpse of the single electron
whirling around in its orbit
and—like Neptune—simply too
distant to see—a green pea
in a green field a half-mile away.

Now in confusion—now
in a wave—a thousand blackbirds
rise and veer above a stubble field—
their wings like obsidian in the sun.

Illusory solidity of the world
and things—the chair I'm on—
its atoms whizzing in arcs,
repelling each other while I sit
musing in this electromagnetic storm—
a chair.

So much space inside an atom,
why can't I reach through this wall?
Is a honeybee
one being, or an element
of one being?

Particles—shadows of waves
in water moving over bright sand.

■ ■ ■

As a child I witnessed a tiny sort of
particle accelerator
in the cold, blue light
of *The Lone Ranger*
on black-and-white TV — a beam
of electrons through a cathode tube
splayed out by a magnet to become
Tonto and Silver crossing
a phosphorescent screen.

Every particle in their bodies represents
the distillation of 100
billion bits from the big bang that
immolated themselves
to become light.

Now even quantum theory agrees,
Form Is Emptiness — mostly.

■ ■ ■

In the glittering domain
of the Summer Triangle — buoyed up
by crickets and frogs —
Vega drags her rhomboid harp
through an isthmus in the Milky Way.

We need our quietest hours to hear Earth
turning night into day —
to feel it gather its waters against
the pull of the moon —

hydrogen holding the waters together,
and we — made mostly of water —

hydrogen molecules drawn to each other —
wrapping up a bit of breathable
air in their hydraulic embrace —
holding me together, and you,
with a little oxygen drawn in.

■ ■ ■

How is it that an atom of hydrogen —
the primary substance of all we know —
can be said to weigh less
than the sum of its parts,
and does that mean the total mass
of the known universe — mostly hydrogen —
would weigh less if we could weigh it
all together at once?

■ ■ ■

Matter appears to be jealous of light —
every particle mad to escape its mass
to be just the light by which we
see our world — without self —
without the distractions of a *you*
and *me*, apparently eternal
like an electron — to have
no substance in which to decay.

The mysterious shore across the great void —
a scary place from all you've heard,
all you've imagined —
never quite clearly in view,
and no one you know
has been there.

And how will you endure your thoughts
in the great dark absence
of everything you've known?

Like the terminals of the battery
in a lamp,
matter and antimatter
cancel each other out
to become light.
Why anything at all should exist
is a riddle we haven't yet solved.

■ ■ ■

Going and coming, the full moon
and rising sun
greet each other
across the plane of the morning.
"Till later," says the moon.
"I'll be along," says the sun.
"I'll be around," says the earth.
"Take your time."

■ ■ ■

Near the pole,
the needle of the magnetic compass
spins like drain water
in its dying frenzy—
finally so close to home.

from THE REVENANT

1971

The Freeze

During the night the wind
shifted to the north
thawing stopped
and snow dust
swirled across the frozen lake
We pulled back into ourselves
the horses were silent
the air too brittle for sound

The house creaks around us
snow hisses
through the trees
We are alone
wrapped in the wind
I light a candle to write this poem
mirrored black in the pane
this storm will not end
this night through our curtain of sleep.

In Michigan

1

Here like the tropics
in summer
in the forest, in the lake
or where the forest ends
a desert of dry grass and stones
over dirt roads, the heat
making you one with
the air
and thus not being one
separate
from that which surrounds you

You rise in early morning
and for an hour
feel yourself
the boy again
in love with summer
the heat, the baking sun
the indolence of planning
nothing for tomorrow

2

I never knew
my father as a young man
forty-four when I was born
fifty as young as I remember him
but in the brown photographs
from "the Great War"
he is young, younger than I

and he calls me
to come back
    a dream that couldn't escape
the businessman
who rose every dawn
to his last years

The Revenant

Near the end
strange light filled the sky
cast no shadows
turned dark trees to light
we knew it was time

Say what has remained unsaid

Dreams
    we make dreams
        sometimes dreams
           are enough

Lightning crossed the clear air
trees stand motionless in the wind

It's colder now

I love you
or wisdom never was

Two Clouds

These songs
may be known
without singing

Five black crows
who steal corn

A pine forest
surrounding
individual trees

A power line leading
to an empty field

One brown apple
sweet beyond tasting

Two clouds
that pass only for clouds

In Ruts and Stars

The season's a matter of weather
not time
though still February
the ground runs soft with mud
the snow, porous and lacy

There is no greater truth
than what I see in this landscape
O ever-returning spring!
each man, this earth
and the way he sees it

I'm sitting here in the woods
It could be a hundred years ago
and I hope
a hundred years to come
that buds will set in a hundred autumns
and snow a hundred winters
a hundred Aprils of violets and lichen
that there *will* be
ever-returning spring
wildness unchanging

It's turning colder
the mud
freezes in ruts and stars

A Mask

How could she know
I cared
more than passing
I spoke
in the guise of study
of "Asphodel, That Greeny Flower," "Among
the Untrodden Ways," of
"Piazza di Spagna, Early Morning" and
Sonnet 14   Browning
In terms of line and metaphor
I talked
that these poems might speak
for what
I couldn't say

from A Year's Turning

WINTER

Through the dark
which gives it light
for us
Polaris
the first we see
is not so far
fifty years
counting by how light will burst
with time, through space

Watching this star
pulls me from this place
my feet lose the ground / I
am nowhere / everywhere

■ ■ ■

I saw a bat
dusting the ceiling
I thought they slept in winter
and killed him with a tennis racket
Shock in my wrist
he spunked like a hollow ball
and faded on the floor
but I did not trust his death

■ ■ ■

An empty tree is filled with stars
and we, tired of dreams
seek new forms
A constellation without name
is waiting to become
and light
flickers from a distant farm

There will be no coming back
to fill with objects
this longing for unknown things

Night
waits to become
all we impose upon her

SPRING

Primary motion
A Cooper's hawk
sails its patterns
circles and dips
hovers and rolls
Wings
form the intent
the hunt of eyes
larger than a man's
followed and fought
against cold silence

■ ■ ■

And how did you
come to be ordinary
though you can't
convince yourself
This field of wild mustard
a sky set in rain
a place for dreaming / a place
to graze your mind
But the gun is lowered
the mind won't graze
Why here
in a field of wild mustard
and how did you come to be ordinary
though you won't
convince yourself

■ ■ ■

All night the rain
driving us through sleep
washes tracks from the road
washes snow from the fields
and somewhere
beyond the rain
the moon
hangs thoughtlessly ornamental
in the sky

SUMMER

Pine trees
and the grasses in a pine forest
like sand vaporized
pulse out a dry smell
as you climb higher
and breathe harder
I stopped to rest
on a fallen tree
I thought of you
gone
and almost suffocated

■ ■ ■

In the moonlight mountains
darker as they are closer
are lighter
    farther away
Clearly / I need
more light
    to see

■ ■ ■

Often these clouds are beautiful
but I
can see storms in them
and sometimes the
sky has
more blue than I can believe

■ ■ ■

After the rain
interrupting our afternoon
            / the woods
floats off a thin smell
like a new day

■ ■ ■

You know you must tell her
and you are resolved;
you have composed the sentences carefully
and you've practiced them
but she'll not help you
will not let you know
she knows

■ ■ ■

The thing about mountains
that from so far away
you can see where you're going
Closer
everything changes / you
can see
        only where you've been

FALL

Afternoon
a slanted light
as on a warm October
all you are
pursuing
something vague of apples
ready growth and still
green bracken   a jay
and the first blue haze
juicy with sleep
weight of leaves
a sadness something
long awaited

■ ■ ■

Fire must have
an edge to cling to
a place
to spread its forces
a spot
    to work away from

■ ■ ■

The duck
wilted in the boat
blood in the bilge
neck strangely twisted
the eye a puncture in flowers

Burn it
burn it all and start again
with less collusion
Each leaf bends into itself
tumbles down and back / spinning
down and back on itself
married to its falling

■ ■ ■

Again frost presses
its patterns
silver fossils on the window
I try seeing beyond
the night is nothing
a background
design of creatures
that never die

For Basil Bunting

He's making something
as a mason piling stone on stone
setting the plan before him

A man passes in the street
he lifts his eyes from the page
to see how he passes
to have been there
and gone on

A foot falls
the frame moves
the moment endures
The mason's trowel
makes rhythm with the mud
laying it on
selecting the stone

Poem to Be Given a Seafaring Title at a Later Date

Falling off from here
a few points
to catch a better wind
and beat the storm
to the breakwater
then turning south
before the wind
running free to a safe harbor
one we can make in this weather
riding crests in a following sea
plunge of bow
deep in the trough and the sweep
of white water down the decks
mast creaking and all lines taut
we hold and sway
carried on the storm that threatens us
Someone is signaling from the beach
the gesture noted and lost
trying to mark
the mouth of a channel we've given up

Waters School Road

A false prophet
the most delicate feather
plucked from a fallen bird
brilliant as a thistle
as the tiniest speck of lavender
you never noticed
at the center of Queen Anne's lace

The road narrows to darkness
along its edge in the deepest green
the fish-white belly of a frog
his legs
sprawled in violent dance
My own faint tracks
the diamond
the nerve in the sole of my shoe

You are here in my hand
or moving under my hand
like a river leaving no trail
or a light growing dim

from Exposures at f/22

A bleached negative
pounding off the snow
it dazzles
Nothing prepares us for this
we have filters to cut the glare but long for night
some corner we can't see around

The light from the window
accentuates her shadows
black crescents
below her breasts
every pore visible
her stomach slopes
to its black triangle

He is feeling the wall
for a streak of sunlight
He is blind and will find it
by its warmth
Above his head
the picture of a crow he painted
It is entirely black
There was no light to surround it

A man in a black cape
tending sheep
    or is it a woman
The sun is rising over the trees

Someone died last night
The sheep are uneasy
and run from the shepherd
The sun is white
the trees are grey
Only one
is distinguishable

The door has the texture
of crusted salt
It is one hundred and thirty years old
and hides nothing
worth the three brass locks
which secure it

Garrapata Beach
black mountains   white plains
and shadows
the mountains cast shadows
larger than themselves
In the foreground a plateau
forming from mist

He is startled
the clarinet held as something forbidden
the cracked wall
the grapevine
his mouth slightly open
eyebrows arched
He is sixteen and resents this intrusion

It is Tuesday in Havana
May Day
"You're some kind of man," she says
looking up
Her arms folded and around her
hats and flags are waving
She wears brass earrings
and a white dress
One eye obscured in shadow

A car is passing
on a silver road
The world around it
is black
It's going nowhere
and comes from nowhere
It is here at this moment   passing

The old woman
walks past the battered wall
A shadow follows her
twisted and huge
It is her shadow
She doesn't want to see it
She keeps her eyes on the ground
humming some tuneless tune

Thirty-nine geese
and the shadows of thirty-nine geese

from DEPARTURE

1973

The Cache

Behind the house   in a field
there's a metal box I buried
full of childhood treasure   a map
of my secret place   a few lead pennies
from 1943
The rest I've forgotten
forgotten even the exact spot
I covered with moss and loam

Now I'm back and twenty years
have made so little difference
I suspect they never happened
this face in the mirror
aged with pencil and putty
I suspect even
the box has moved as a mole would move
to a new place long ago

Notes from the Underground

I enter the book
amazed to discover
the destruction of happiness
At times I think I'm a reasonable man
though I have no use for reason
Faces intrude saying, *I'm to be considered*
Stay at home   Don't take a chance
It rains when you least expect it
No one relies on tomorrow
a proverb   the interpretation
the words of the wise   their dark sayings
like giving everything you own away
relieved to discover
it was never yours

from THE CHINESE POEMS

1978

Dripping from the eaves   everything melting
clearheaded this morning in the mist
drifting like life from the ice

The order and disorder of that order

"Nothing is so important"
The way we read that
defines our vision

We had better leave it
"Nothing is"

from Letters to a Distant Friend

1

Nothing seems to get any better
I have given up waiting for more
Once we had youth on our side
full of promise
Now we are what we are
and struggle with one aging mind
to climb the wall
we no longer believe is there

2

For months we live a day's trip apart
absorbed in writing flowers for the void
What are they to us
but orphaned children
What are these days that won't come again
but moments we labor
to preserve our loneliness

5

Another winter morning
I'm expecting your call
I stand close to the window and watch
my breath form a rose on the glass
I scratch your name on it
then wipe it away with my sleeve
listening for your tires
to crunch through the ice on the drive
I notice how snow glistens on the pine boughs

that there's no wind at all
It's too cold for my walk
Nothing dares disturb this stillness
I know you aren't coming
I press my cheek to the window
The telephone rings
My breath forms a rose on the glass

9

Happiness is only one condition
Fools search for it
If you can't love ashes
what is the sense of burning wood
Too much wine is a pleasure and a pain
If we were together too long
we would fight
A little sadness like salt
enhances the flavor

11

I have been sick and have lost my voice
We haven't talked for weeks
Tonight you called
and for the first time spoken
you said "I love you"
After all these years these words between friends
I couldn't speak
but you heard me

13

Each moment we recognize is gone
and so too the days
we try to pin down with words

which are only moments given sound
I live
trying to catch moonlight with the paper
on which I send you this night

14

Looking back
at my footprints in the snow
I wonder
Who is this me
who longs to answer this question
this me
who walked here alone
    impudent authority
so far from home

15

Though tonight we are happy
we will come to grief
What of it
If we look for something endless
our lives will be endless looking
Why not settle for this
new wood on the fire
the moon in love
with the new-fallen snow

19

The crescent moon appears in the west
Taking leave, we first see it
though it's been with us all day
like the sound of a bell
before it's struck

or the sound of your voice
when I'm far away

20

Even with a continent between us
we hear the same music
rare, even among those who never part
If you die before me
I'll trace these letters with my finger
in the air
so the birds can fly through them
and translate this song

29

Each day we are faced with having done nothing
no matter what we do
Our lives like the wake of a boat
close behind us
Better not to look from too far away
Only at getting these words down now
then to split wood   then to eat lunch
then mail this letter
then to look again at the void

30

I begin this letter
writing the date at the top of the page
like an incantation
for some unnamed thing to take life
Why call it April
when a sudden snow stills the peepers
and I turn from windows where
frost blares against the new green rye

or the sixth day
breaking always into convenient shares
and a year to count our progress

34

I thought of you
as I dropped this Grey Wulff at the base of a stump
I watched the minute dapple of water around it
I waited for some nameless creature to rise
While in the trees above, two herons were resting
a kingfisher rattled and skimmed the surface
and a turtle slid off a log
like the author of a dream
slipping into the day

35

There are nights
I don't know what to do
with my arms
nights it would be a pleasure
to take them off
to stack them by the bed
and swim like a dolphin
through this dreamless sea

41

A December evening and as it grows dark
the fog becomes pearly above the snow
around the black trees, between my palate and teeth
like a baleen whale I squeeze it out
half-believing some magic will stick to my tongue
when next I speak
these moments between us, a thousand miles

of fog, darker with each increment of the earth
my daughter calling and my dog drives me mad
chewing on a bone, the abrasive crackle of the fire
the unbearable stillness of these words
knowing that now this will never change

42

Each night I build a fire
giving large chunks of oak to the flames
resinous pine and fragrant cedar
moments of this life
I throw in my guitar of white maple
my desires of white flesh
hopes, memories, dreams
ping in the flames
leaving no trace
Wood is wood, ash is ash
fire is fire

from SNOW ON THE BACKS OF ANIMALS

1986

In the Winter Dark

The door half open
in a dark hallway, roller skate
on the stairs, marbles
scattered on the kitchen floor,
hold those impenetrable silences
between father and son
as the two drive home in the winter dark.

Do these smoldering logs, waiting
to be stirred back to flame,
become the compulsion to build cathedrals,
pyramids, tombs,
the great buried silos of North Dakota?

The shadow of a man trudges over the field.

One of those logs in the fireplace
suddenly takes off on its own,
burning furiously
through a pocket of air.

The light fails so early.
The hemlocks grow heavy.

The shadow drives an image of the man before it.

The Way Back

At the edge of the woods, I take off my skis and
sit back against a tree, enjoying the midwinter
sun. The sky, a blue bowl after weeks of grey
and listless snow. All day now I've been watched,
an intruder, lumbering through the dark trees. I
look but can't see the eyes watching me. I give
myself to the warmth on my face. I close my eyes,
awaken to the blood of my eyelids and see fiery
eruptions on the surface of the sun. Still,
the watchers come closer, uncertain I'm not
some kind of deep-blue fungus growing on the tree.
Soon I can see through their eyes, many eyes all
together, and through the eyes of the hawk turning
above, a white spot against the sky, a blue spot
against the snow, borne away by some instinct
from this *thing* I have been.

Speaking to Horses

for Bill Dickinson

From my childhood I remember achingly clear winter
nights on the hay of a sledge, riding up snow-
covered country roads, singing, shouting, jumping
off and running alongside to impress the girls,
and under it all, the groundtone of his voice gentling
the horses. And I remember the sight of him across
our north pasture, following his team, the reins
across his shoulders, one foot in the furrow and
one on the newly turned ridge, like an ancient
traveler in our time, pursuing a life technology
and economics had declared defunct. But not for
him. He refused to be part of that progress-driven
consensus in its race for prosperity and oblivion.
For him, the horses were huge, muscular children
who sometimes needed a firm hand, but never an
angry one, a life in the present, of caring and
slow time.

Two weeks ago, pneumonia ganged up with a
rare blood disease, and he died. There was standing-
room only at his funeral: farmers in suspenders,
their weather-browned necks confined in white collars,
and many people my own age who must also, as children,
have heard him talking to his horses and learned
something about patience and gentleness. Outside,
a team of Belgians, the horses of a friend, stood
harnessed to a black box-carriage in the hot September
sun. Occasionally they pawed the pavement and
nuzzled each other as befit the occasion in their

being horses. Two drivers in black livery and
top hats with black sashes waited to take him on
his last carriage ride. Traffic backed up all
through town as the procession moved with the same
mindful slowness with which he'd lived.

Up ahead, as the carriage turned down the
cemetery lane, we could see the giant horses ambling
through the shadows of the trees.

Return

I

September, and the acorns come crashing
from branch to branch, whistling through the leaves,
all around the dark house
like tiny planets cast out from space.
Not an hour goes by but I wonder
at the weight of sadness that pulls them down.
I kindle the first fire
and pull up my chair and sit close.

A blind man, they say,
can smell the night coming on.

2

Autumn moans through the cabin door,
sounding of winter and darkness and sleep
and something more certain.
In the north wind,
the lake flows south like a river
past an opening in the trees.
I watch it for hours drifting
through huddled fields and creaking woods,
past empty farms
where armies have camped and moved on.

The View from the Pasture

The old horse walks to the edge of the
pasture and stands stretching his neck
over the fence, as if he could see through
the falling snow, smell the ungrazed
grass matted under the ice or the frozen
orchard across the road.

There is no color in the earth or sky.
Viewing his world so long from this ground,
he knows the past and future as a windmill,
a tractor, a pump arm that beckons.

December

Night has been falling
all afternoon. I'm not concerned
with what comes or goes.

Below my feet snakes coil
together. Not one bird is flying.
Not one fish cares about ice.

The last flies buzz, slow and clumsy.
They stumble across my knuckles
and I let them. They are old

and the year is old, and
I haven't lived
a more perfect day.

Homecoming

You return home
to find your house no longer there.
The trees have grown back
and the toe of a boot you received for Christmas
protrudes through the loam of your floor.
The door you locked in the morning
is the space between twilight
and the serialized stars.
Your wife, your children,
their wings extended,
circle the treetops
and sing indifferently of what you were.

The Sanatorium

He wasn't permitted inside
but would stand out in the yard
among the towering oaks
and wave to his father at the window.
They would wave to each other
until it seemed silly, like saying
"door" a hundred times.

Then suddenly his father would be gone
and he would find himself
waving at the black window, feeling foolish,
hoping no one was watching
the fluttering of his hand
like a bird in the air.

Burning the Last Logs of Winter

A spring wind rattles the window,
and the farmer turns fitfully under the moon.

Tubers sprout below the frost line.
Soon the fields will be plowed.

What snow is left whitens the gullies
like sweeps of canvas waiting for paint.

I awake and my parents are together again
as if they'd discovered that death is a dream.

Journal Entry

Though supposedly spring,
snow is falling for the third straight day.

Two weeks ago my father died,
and I'm with him now
more than when he was living.
I see him with my grandparents,
thinner,
in a white linen suit and Panama hat.
He dances with my mother
or stands in the back of a Model T truck,
in his uniform, just back from France.

Then, sitting on his knee,
unjustly spanked:
my lips protrude, and my skin
forms a cauliflower of rage.

I follow him like an old black dog.
Yabut, he calls me.
Yeah, but, I say, *but it isn't fair.*

I feel the cold
through the soles of my shoes,
the peepers sing from the pond,
a few more flakes in the air.

For Randall Jarrell

for Gretel Ehrlich

A man struck by lightning
is seldom appeased by house current.
The bolt that steals vision or
restores it, splits the young poplar,
hurls thunder over the roof,
makes widows of farmwives
and ashes of the barn.

The wild geese never die; the lilacs
reappear each May, and the night sky
continues its imperturbable dance.

Tuesday in Key West

It wasn't as it might've been had it rained.
I would've sat in the Cuban bar drinking coffee,

watching the people in the street getting wet
and not caring.

I wouldn't care, and they wouldn't care.

At this latitude rain, by itself, doesn't matter.
It comes like sweat,

and dries in its own good time.
People die or leave town,

and nothing changes but the moon
and what the tide brings in, bright men-of-war,

oily bubbles a child might've blown,
a suitcase full of sand, a lawn chair,

anything Earth might offer you. Three girls
lying topless, six breasts pooling into themselves.

Six perfect nipples, two hard as buttons,
two peaked like pink custard,
two dark as knots in varnished pine.

Parzival

He dreams of her head thrown back on the pillow,
her cries of relief from so much longing.

Her breasts slope to him,
a valley leading home,

no longer aware
of being a man or a woman,

only blood on the snow,
and a bird is flying.

The Third Week of July

Chaff gets down my shirt, and the cut stalks of
the bale ends rub my forearms raw. Always the
hottest day of the summer, always, with clouds
getting dark in the west, when the wagon is borrowed
to haul hay from Monette's. We used to put up
our own, but farming's an expensive hobby. The
elevator rigged to the loft of the barn, the wagon
hitched to the truck, and every year the same
reminiscence, work and wages now, compared to when
we were young, though I went to school with Monette's
daughter, and his youth and mine were in different
worlds. "Kids don't want to work that hard anymore,
no matter what you pay," he says. "They ain't got
the patience." But for Monette and me it's easier
now, past the agony of feeling our lives getting
away from us. We develop a rhythm, building the
load, knowing that though the years seem short,
the day is long, and there's nowhere else to be.

My daughter, Tamara, pulls the bales from
the rick, and Monette and I heave them up to Warren
who interlocks the rows. We try to keep count
but get lost and have to refigure it, a hundred
on the wagon, fifty on the truck. Two loads should
hold us the winter. A dollar-fifty a bale this
summer; he could get three if he held it till the
snow comes, but that's not his game he tells us.
"Turned down a man from Indiana, wanted five thousand
bales just like that." He snaps his fingers, then

wipes the sweat with his sleeve. "But it's a one-
time deal. I got to service my regular customers."

It's nearly midafternoon when I pay Monette
and we pull out slow, gentling the load down his
drive. We take our time. Once Warren and I dumped
half a wagon on Main Street and had to rebuild
it in blocked traffic and unwelcome advice from
the sidewalk. Play-farmers exposed. We turn the
vent windows all the way round, hoping to find
something cool in the air. Our shirts stick to
our backs, and the heat slows down in our heads.
Tamara has a crush on Warren and teases him about
his girlfriends, testing this new woman beginning
to take over her name. She slugs him on the shoulder
as a sign of affection, and then, to be democratic,
ruffles my hair.

In the loft, Warren and I strain to keep pace
with the bales Tamara and her brother, Frank, feed
the elevator. The heat up here throbs like a drum.
The elevator's clatter pushes us on. I catch the
bales and pitch them to Warren in what becomes
a machine-like dance. We keep space for air between
the bales and the wall. Barns have exploded in
heat like this. We keep space around the windows
and keep them open. Sweat gets in our eyes, and
our throats ache with the dust and chaff. For days
we'll find fragments in our navels and ears. The
loft shrinks as the hay closes in around us.

Finally, I turn for a bale that isn't there
and look down and see that the wagon is cleared.
My son and daughter are bombarding each other with
the broken leaves. Warren and I wonder at their
energy as we collapse on the mound we have built,
feeling righteous and empty. I recall something
Thoreau said, that nothing is so unprofitable as
talking with farmers because they always fall back
on their virtue. Maybe so. If I were to speak
now I'd say something like, "Yes, the earth is
good," and so I keep silent. "The Man who pretends
to be a modest enquirer into the truth of a self
evident thing is a Knave," Blake said. I laugh
at the way other men's words dribble out of me.
Warren thinks I'm laughing at our transformation
into hayseeds, at the straw he's poked up his nose,
and we laugh together over that and our agreement
about how easy a few cold beers will go down. We
hear the first rumble of thunder in the west. I
feel the stiffness already in my shoulders as I
get up and walk to the hay door. At the far end
of the pasture the horses graze, their noses deep
in the succulent grass.

Thousand Moon Lake

There are Indian mounds, two or three,
said to border this lake,
but I haven't found them;
rain that fills the trees,
earth that holds them spongy,
remnants of ancient barbed wire
grown halfway through their trunks.

In winter it seems a frozen pasture.
Only its flatness and irregular shape
would make you suspect
that under the snow, there's more.

Except for a silo on the hill
above the trees on the western shore,
almost obscured by leaves,
or a jet dividing the sky
at noon,
the Indians, one hundred years
before Christ, had yet
to build their mounds.

Birds feed and die at its edge,
herons nesting in tamarack,
a snake crawls into the nest
or dangles from the claw of a hawk,
the soft aggressive slither,
the heron gliding at sunset.

This spring, two horses drowned,
great children plunging
through the fluted ice,
the splash and struggle;
the broken water reforms,
clouds part, the sun appears,
a kingfisher flies low
and rattles out his call.

I drift in my boat
with no story,
connected to nothing but the shore.

Wind flues in the pines overhead,
dapples the face of the water,
alters my line
as I cast to small fish,
dreaming
on beds of old leaves,

and catch the image of the fisherman,
no more observer than observed,
no more observed than rings
pooling at the exposed roots
of the maple where a life has risen
to dance with the bones of my wrist.

The Line

A day worth losing
flows by with the river.

The brown skin of my hand
turns over a line,
gathers slack from the current.

Each day there are messages
we ignore by the stream.

The line moves
as stars flow,
in patterns a life goes by.

No song, but in my ear,
lead, fire, rain,
tar and couch grass,
the picture in a million grey dots.

The lines of my hand
flow off the edge,
rivers of the world
irretrievably lost,

    discipline   discipline
channeling my life
in the music of the world.

I have opened this line
to the threads of a milkpod,
spunk smell of loam,
effulgence of the brain,
the idle lust of my eyes.

This October in Fremont, Michigan

The smoke of burning leaves intoxicates the
sleepy towns of the recession. Another autumn,
no good news, and winter storms coming on.
He rocks on his porch, not unconcerned, but
what is there to be done? He can't clear-
cut the yard to stoke an oil stove or bale
his lawn for the dog. His measure and level
languish in the hall. He starts awake with
an aimless joy, bearing from sleep the heft
of a hammer rocking in the bones of his hand,
the last nail-thud alive in his ear. The
clean scream of his saw fades off down the
street, and he isn't quite sure whose street
this is. His wife's been riding his nerves.
He's sleeping later every day, and his lunch
pail gapes at the kitchen wall, a small tug
far from the sea.

Afterwords

We say *tree*
for the object that isn't there.

We say *I love you,*
acknowledging the failure
of whatever there was
to speak for itself.

We say *God did it;*
we mistrust everything.

You read these lines.
You think of something profound.
You pay too much for the ticket
and miss the plane.

The Man Who Doesn't Change

The wind abides nowhere.
Or it isn't the wind;
it is the motion of the mind
through pine boughs.

In 1948 in Chicago

My father swerved to miss a paperboy, turned the
wrong way up a one-way street and got nailed by
the cop on the corner. He never had a chance to
explain, and it wouldn't have made any difference.
Maybe the cop had been pondering a nightmare, his
wife moaning under the dance instructor two floors
down or his daughter threatening to leave home
if she couldn't go up to Wisconsin for the weekend
with the defensive backfield and a couple of other
friends. It isn't easy being a father; I realize
that now, those dark silences I caused, those
looks of resentment, ways I had of putting the
guilt on him. Maybe we're all that way, and he
was thinking about that when the newsboy stepped
off the curb to sell a paper, never intending to
dart into the street. "Where're you from, anyway?"
the cop yelled back, after the lecture, after telling
him to beat it. "Fremont," my father shouted,
feeling his small-town pride as he said it, certain
the cops in Fremont were never this blind. "I
thought so!" The cop heaved his shoulders
and turned away in disgust. In every thought I've
had since he died, my father has forgiven me.

Adumbratio

In his death, my father has been wandering
through the forest. He enters a clearing
and stops to ponder the living sweep of the
sky. He holds back in the shadows, so as
not to be noticed, avoiding the probing fingers
of light. Sometimes he takes the form of
a bird or a pebble or the wind's high rejoinder
in the pines. When clouds build over the
afternoon, his shadow dissolves into moss,
lichen, the dry carpet of leaves. I walk
eastward along the bed of a stream where
a stream once was or will be.

The Life of the Fox

This morning, before a strong south wind moved in
to clear the lake of winter, I saw a fox trying to
find his way off the ice, testing the edges,
retreating again and again until he found a spot
that would hold, that would get him back into the
forest.

A tree. A perfect tree. A large oak catching and
releasing the wind. A hundred years of life, a
thousand board feet that could become an ark, an
oak bridge, an armoire for a queen, but never
again a beautiful tree.

Is it possible the fox may be my father, returned
to innumerable lives, none of them better or worse
in the judgment of the fox, who chooses without
question whatever is given?

Should I save the frog from the snake gliding
toward the edge of the lake? Should I save the
sparrow from my cat, save the chicken from my
table, stewing in its broth of wine, tarragon, and
garlic?

I can't save the deer. I start with each shot and
run to the window and realize what I hear is only
target practice or an orchard gun or at worst a
death quicker than by wild dogs or starvation. I
can't save my friend from the cancer distending
his liver or the woman who cared for me from the

years that have worn her away, much less the
starving of Africa to whom I send money or those
in love with ignorance who will never open up to
their lives.

Eleven years since my father died to the day I
found a fox with his leg in a trap, waiting like
someone's red dog to be unchained, until I got
close. I pinned him down with a log and sprang
him free as he snarled and bared his fangs at
whatever it was that caused him pain. The trapper
followed my tracks and threatened to kill me.
"If that's what you've decided to do," I said,
the .357 in his holster, the cold blue-black of a
cobra at close range, and I desperately did not
want to die.

Three beautiful skulls in my cabin: turtle skull,
deer skull, long-horned steer, white and perfect
structures on which no life can be rebuilt. Add
to them the skull of the dog who sleeps on my
couch, of the cat who sleeps on the rug at my
feet, skull of the woman whose head rests on the
pillow next to mine, the skull I feel with my
fingers through my cheeks, so white and perfect
and on which no life can be rebuilt.

Snow on the Backs of Animals

There is a peacefulness
when snow falls like this, over everything,
and keeps on falling, windlessly,
on fence rails and ditches, made level now,
filling the upturned pail in the yard,
wiping the field clear of corn stubble, even
smothering the news and anyone
attempting to reach us.

A man walks out on a night like this
and the darkness weighs down his arms.
He forgets his purpose, stumbles,
gives up whatever it was he wanted,
and enters the bodies of his friends,
growing deep and luminous.

from A LAST BRIDGE HOME

1992

Someone

Someone is clearing a ditch for the rains
when they come,
burning leaves withered under the snow.

Smoke grazes the horizon,
pressing the sun into a confident sphere.

An unmuffled motorbike
is tearing down a section road,
winding up and shifting
its anger on the spring.

Someone is listening over newly plowed fields.
Someone is waiting for the stars to shine,
someone grieving a past that wasn't lived,
someone watching the clouds
roll up into a range of low hills.

Why I Don't Take Naps in the Afternoon

It occurs to you that everything has gone awry.
It all should have turned out differently.
Everyone has chosen the wrong mate. Everything
that should have been spoken has been held back.
It's not the world but the residue of what the
world intended. It all makes sense to you, now
that your mistresses have gotten married. Eternity.
We are living in eternity.

The clouds break open, the sun about to set.
Nothing you can do about it. You walk from your
hotel, down rain-washed streets, glistening in places.
The cafés are closed, or you feel they should be closed.
The life in them doesn't concern you.
Exhausted by certainty, nothing concerns you
but the pull of the river, the dark
brown current swirling in eddies,
drawn too powerfully to what it doesn't know,
not to turn back on itself.
You watch a glassy ring, watch it
ripple then curl, then lost in the stream.
And you notice the pavement under your feet,
the hardness of it, and
the iron rail under your arms.

A Last Bridge Home

Einstein said of his Theory,
It's too beautiful not to be true.
And I'm riding this train
the last miles home
though there was no train to my hometown
in this life that I can remember.
Still, someone waits on the platform
as I thunder out of the forest
and through the swamp at the edge of town.
Someone who paces,
who glances at the depot clock
and strains to see up the tracks,
that first glimpse of smoke
as I rattle over this last bridge home.

This Harmony

The dying buffalo on the Serengeti
gratefully receives
the spear we plunge through his heart,
as do the hyenas, vultures, and jackals.
They descend on him like a magician's cloak,
and a day later
nothing remains but a blood spot on the grass
and one hank of hair from the end of his tail.
We look up to watch the sun drop
below the escarpment
and to ponder how one life has flown
or loped or trotted off,
a hundred different ways,
and how the grass takes its moisture
any way it can.

from TRYING TO CATCH THE HORSES

1999

Trying to Catch the Horses

When I give up and turn my attention
to the purr of the grass, the clatter of the aspen,
the clouds lifting off Mt. Teewinot,
I become a curious god, a tar baby,
a clump of grass they must graze.

I reach up and touch the blue with my fingers,
not just the air above my head
but the sky itself as far as it goes.

The Trees, the Grass, the Leaves, the River

> *The desire to be a creator, to give birth, [is] nothing*
> *without the thousandfold consent of things and animals.*
>
> RILKE

Would these things I came to praise
be pleased if I read them my poems?
Or would I feel foolish in their presence,
reciting what I've made of their incomparable lives?

If I came to this meadow to exalt them
would I clear my throat for their attention
and then be unable to speak?

Would I be wounded by the silence of the stones,
the resolve of the river,
not even pausing to listen, the falcon
intent on a life in the air, the fox
trotting off at the sound of my voice?

Or would they be secretly pleased
and reward me with their mute applause,
simply being more what they are?

Would the prairie dog come out of her den to scold me,
the crane clack and wallop her articulate wings,
the wind pick up and roar in the willows,
to absolve me in this chorus
of their amplified song?

A Tree on the Prairie in Mid-October

Something about the single aspen
I photographed a dozen times this fall,
hidden from view in sage and grass
on the far slope of the hill
I can see from my bedroom window.

Of those who walked with me,
no one took notice. I don't know why
I am drawn to this gnome-like tree —
the way its heart-shaped leaves
enliven the sun perhaps,
a little more gold each day.

Something not only of itself
comes out of the tree when I see it,
something not me that I am.

Our lives are short in the middle
and long at both ends.

How strange to give up being alone.

Walking Out Alone

Have you ever doubted that the basement stairs
go deeper than the basement,
that the desire you ignore is desiring you?

That plaintive look on the faces of dogs
we take to express so much more longing
than they probably ever intended.

Beyond the meadow is a greater meadow
and beyond the trees, more trees.

In the late winter sun, these hard, little pebbles
cast hard, little shadows on the road.

A Time of the Hoppers

It was August,
time of the leaping and crackling grass,
dry end of summer, of fires
and the ripening wheat.

Along the rivers the hoppers leap out with abandon,
with joy and no thought of ever coming down.
Sweeping the bank on the ride of their life,
they soon become the life of the roseate,
speckled, and ravenous trout, a transformation
they never imagined.
Or maybe they had.

Who am I to speculate about the wisdom of an arthropod
I merely mimic with feathers on a hook?
Who am I to question this glorious transformation

I hold now a moment in the current
and let go?

On My Walk

I wonder
if I'm any less lonely than I ever was.

Wildflowers, in this case
the yellow arrowroot,
wait for me in the fields.

The long-needled pine has secrets it will keep
till the breeze rises. And the breeze
has stories for the pine to translate.

The roots of the sage almost trip me,
and the marsh hawk swoops low
to show me her bright wings.

She forgets she has done this before.

The fox on the hillside,
across the slim ravine, watches
to see where I might be going
and what it is I might do.

This doesn't concern her, except
that everything concerns her,
and concerns me, too. I suspect

that she is always watching
and almost never lonely.

Counting Treasures

My dog lies on the threshold,
and her ears are never still.
If I were deaf I could read
just watching them
flag like velvet semaphores,
saying, *breeze, rain, bees,*
laughter from next door.

The Bear on Main Street

What made the man kill this bear?
His truck, across which the bear's body lies,
tells me it wasn't to feed his family
or because his children were cold.

The bear has beautiful black feet, delicate
almost, like the soles of patent-leather slippers,
and the wind riffles the surface of its fur
with the sheen of water in the autumn sun.

The bear looks as if it might only be sleeping,
but its tongue lags from its mouth, and the man
has wrapped it with stout twine and bound it
to the bed of his truck,
as if he were afraid it might speak.

Three teenage boys pull their pickup to the curb.
One of the boys guesses what the bear must weigh.
Another wants to know how many shots it took,
and the third boy climbs down. He strokes its nose and forehead.
He traces the bear's no longer living skull
with the living bones of his fingers
and wonders by what impossible road
he will come to his father's country.

Tarawa

they did not hear
the singing of the reefs long enough
and perhaps never touched the islands, those wreaths of
*   brilliance and perfume,*
except to die

PABLO NERUDA

This is a story about what happened in '43 —
there are twenty thousand twenty-seven
stories like this — about the hit I took
through the knee on the way in,
wading over the long reef,
about the color of the water
around me, how it blended
with bits of broken coral
and blood from other knees, like a great soup
stirred up from leftovers, how the frightened bonefish,
trapped by the tide,
shot through our legs. We never thought
of fish in the sea and how
this was their home though not their war,
and not ours either, though
we were swimming in it.

South of Marrakech

He remembers the car on its smashed roof,
wheels up, like a sleeping dog,
the dark, almost colorless rocks,
before the heat of the morning,
the men in their musty djellabas
around the small fire, cooking coffee
by the road to Ait-Ben-Haddou,
the bodies half covered, the surprisingly delicate
foot of the woman and the blue-stained arm of the man,
blood sticky in the cupped palm of his hand,
coffee coming to a boil in the tall brass pot,
the man with the milky eye gesturing
toward the cloudless sky
when we stopped because we were strangers
to see what there was we might do.

Flight

She told me no man
ever pleased her this way
and asked sweetly
that I do it again.

Of course I was really pleasing myself,
the way raptors are pleased
by the air moving under their wings,
only more so
when the wind they create buffets back
with its own life,
and the trailing feathers thrill
to this unbidden lift.

Adrift

There was nothing he could do now, nothing
to provide for his journey. And so
doing nothing was easy.

The boat without power would go
where the current took it, the falling tide
drawing him out to where
the horizon would be.

                      But the light from the clouds
hammered it smooth like fine metal
hammered into leaf on an anvil
between ocean and what the sky might bring.

The woman he would never see again,
a creature as the sharks are
creatures, and the tern alone so high,
a spirit alone for all he could see.

And he noticed a large green turtle
lolling in the swells,

how he would tell
of its large dispassionate eye,

how it calmed him to someone
he had the chance to be someday.

The Cool Earth

It's noontime on a summer day sometime around 1948. Box-cars are standing on the tracks, doors open, waiting for the rest of their loads. But it's noontime now and the lift-truck drivers are resting. Hay bales stretch out over half the field. The farm-hands are resting under the large maple along the fence line, their shirts wet from the morning's hauling, and with the light breeze there in the shade, the rough cotton feels cold against their backs and ribs. I come home, hot from play. My mother has made me an egg-salad sandwich, and the screen door whaps on its spring. Our dog is resting on the cool earth of the fox-hole he's scooped out against the foundation of the house. My father stops to speak to him before he comes in. My father groans as he imagines he would groan if he were the dog, stretching there to his greeting, stiff legged on the cool black earth in the shadow of the kitchen roof. He carries the jacket of his seer-sucker suit on his arm, and the morning's mail in his hand. There is a knowing, beyond but not apart from this. I hear the *braang* of the spring as it stretches, though there is no slap, as my father eases the door shut behind him. He kisses my mother and drops the mail on the counter. "It's hot," he says, but he clearly enjoys it. He's as happy as I am that it's a hot summer day in our little town and that it's noontime sometime around 1948.

Spirit Harness

But before I set foot on it, I realize
I am already on the other side.

Though I can never cross it, the bridge
is there like a finger pointing at the moon,

though the finger itself gives off no light.

Psalm

All my dead are with me.
All my dead are at ease,
free of time and what never may be.
All my dead are at peace with each other.
They will never change their minds.
They forgive me whatever I feel
needs forgiveness, and blame
what I think needs blame.
They are sunlight come to comfort me.
They lead me on the trail of my life's work.
In my hand I see my father's hand,
holding this pen.
My mother's eyes, finally free of longing,
gaze at me from the mirror.
When I stand they look up
to see where I'm going.
They can't see far through the tall grass,
but they see the tall grass,
and they smile to see it moving behind me.

Dust

This crumbling brick has no fear of death,
doesn't know whether it's coming or going.

Particles compressed make a brick,
make the brick, like me,
an assemblage.

Speck of dust, who are you?
Never again will I shake out the rag,
determined to be rid of you once and for all.

Where have you been, my love?
And where will I meet you tomorrow?

What do you think?

BOOK TITLE: _____

COMMENTS: _____

_____

_____

_____

OUR MISSION:

Poetry is vital to language and living. Copper Canyon Press publishes extraordinary poetry from around the world to engage the imaginations and intellects of readers.

Thank you for your thoughts!

Can we quote you? ☐ yes ☐ no

☐ Please send me a catalog full of poems and email news on forthcoming titles, readings, and poetry events.

☐ Please send me information on becoming a patron of Copper Canyon Press.

NAME: _____

ADDRESS: _____

CITY: _____ STATE: _____ ZIP: _____

EMAIL: _____

MAIL THIS CARD, SHARE YOUR COMMENTS ON FACEBOOK OR TWITTER,
OR EMAIL POETRY@COPPERCANYONPRESS.ORG

Copper Canyon Press
A nonprofit publisher dedicated to poetry

 CopperCanyonPress.org

BUSINESS REPLY MAIL

FIRST-CLASS MAIL   PERMIT NO. 43   PORT TOWNSEND WA

POSTAGE WILL BE PAID BY ADDRESSEE

Copper Canyon Press
PO Box 271
Port Townsend, WA 98368-9931

Advice from the Burglar

Sometimes the most audacious attempt
is the only way in,
when all the other windows are shuttered
and only that one on the street,
so naked in the light,
no one would think to defend it.

Go about this as if you belong here.
Bring your ladder.
Bring music and all your tools.
And make a neat job of it.
Talk with anyone who stops.
Speak of the weather and how you'd rather be sailing.

The tricky part comes once you're inside.
Others may have tried this before you.
The house seems familiar, and the owner
may have left something for you.

It may, in fact, be what you're seeking.

The Favorite Child

*My mother cries because I am old in my time
and because I will never get old enough to be old in hers!*
CÉSAR VALLEJO

When your mother, in the pale moonlight,
bent down to your cradle and whispered
This child is my favorite,
you might have heard another voice
singing like a kettle of steam,

*And I'll caress him when he pleases me
and teach him everything I know, almost,
and make him love the things I love.*

*And he will be my longing
for a place I'll never be,
and I will be the smile
of a woman he'll never know.*

*And I will eat this child, and he will satisfy
the hunger in me. Maybe.
And I will eat him slowly, a little
at a time and make him last
my whole long life, and even a little longer
so that I can go on eating
even when I have no stomach.*

Quite by Chance

I find myself by a lake
where I discover my divorced wife,
long dead now,
spent her summers as a child,
long before I knew her name.

I loved that little girl
I never knew. I must have
because I later loved the woman
those summers became.

I must still love her in some way or why
does this knowing become such sweet pain —
something I think I want to tell the little girl
who of course has been well warned
not to speak to strangers.

A Face at the Window

What they want of me is that I gently remove the appearance
of injustice about their death — which at times
slightly hinders their souls from proceeding onward.

RILKE

Old sorrows that lurk around the house,
feeling for a crack in the siding,
are like a fire we think has gone cold,
the embers ground into ashes
but the ashes still glow.

They wait in the dark till we're distracted,
then slip in around a casement
where we've let the caulking go.

We sit them down at our table
without thinking. We warm them
with our desires; we tell them our favorite stories
and urge them to drink our best wine.

We embrace them and they
whisper the names that have wronged us.
We feel them breathe in our ear
and grow dizzy with their love of injustice.

They form to our bodies like worn leather
till we hardly sense them at all,
only that the night has grown thicker
and the lamplight strains at the bulb.

I think of Orpheus coming out of that darkness
with nothing but tears to show for his travail,
that what we still long for
longs to be let go,
like that fleeting but unmistakable flavor in the air
just before it starts to rain.

Plum Rain

The final plum in the kitchen bowl,
overripe, its skin even a little withered,
but sweet, so sweet it breaks in two
as I bite into it. The pit, like the soul
that isn't inside the body
but still is the body,
pops out into my fingers
and the short stem
I fish from between my teeth
points back to the tree,
the sun, and the rain
where the plum and I
began this fatal longing.

My Father's Fields

September 1918

They looked like blackbirds, my father said,
that first burst of shrapnel,
spiraling up in autumn flight,
and at first that's what he thought they were,
their glossy wings catching the sun
as they wheeled in the morning sky.

There was that moment of beauty,
the glint of it,
in that first day on the Meuse-Argonne
before the earth came off its perch,
as if they had offended it somehow,
or that's the thought he had, he said,
the earth rising up over every stored transgression,
and what had they done to bring this on?

Later it was all the dead horses,
the field before the river strewn with horses,
and his friend, Carl Johnson,
sleeping off the numbness of battle,
at peace almost,
but for the way his leg wrapped up behind him,
and the too-wide smile
of the bloody mouth across his neck,
Carl playing dead among the horses; he thought
of Carl with his Belgians at the county fair.

Ninety thousand horses moving up the roads at night.
He'd never imagined so many horses

in the history of the world,
or so many men in their silent march,
imagining no longer, the September morning
as they looked out on the manicured stubble
of the burnt-gold fields
and the still, green trees in the haze
along the river.

These few things he noted in his journal,
though he spoke to me only of the horses,
the things people said, and the newly shorn fields.

The trees along the river are what I see
when I think my father's thoughts,
not the fiery sky, the tangled wire,
the splintered forest or all the dead horses,
but those fields shorn of wheat,
as his father's fields would be in September.

Wild Horses

Out my window, wild horses. Or they aren't really wild; they are my neighbor's horses wandering over the unfenced fields. They are wild to me. They touch something long before minoxidil and the World Wide Web. *To see you naked is to see the earth swept clean of horses.* But not really; swept clean *for* horses maybe. My neighbor's daughter rolls down the car window to ask if I've seen her horses. One of them is black and white. Something in me wants her to ask me to saddle up and help her corral them. To ride down the scree slopes of canyons, to come into a wild country where the centaur still lives, to ride together till *the hills run away.* I tell her I saw them move off over Teton Ridge, southeast. Good luck I tell her. She backs on the shoulder and waves as she turns toward home. Wild horses. One of them a paint with a black fiddle head. I look back over my shoulder. I can smell the riders coming. I wait for them on the ridge above the coulee. I will let them come closer, let them almost believe they can catch me.

from **A PRIMER ON PARALLEL LIVES**

2007

In Praise of Humberto Tapia

I cup my hands around the last bright speck
and blow gently to keep it alive, an ember
of oak log, pared from a tree
Humberto Tapia rescued with his artful pruning,
from stifling mistletoe and Spanish moss,
and the unleavened abundance that
drags it down, a life like my own
from which too little has been let go.

Now I see this coal
as a fallen star,
one bright thing in a field of night,
curious about the darkness
and the world kneeling down to it,
using its breath to keep it glowing.

Tracking the Moment

The place where I stopped last night is far away;
and tomorrow, tonight will be last night.

YANG WAN-LI 1127–1206

A million stars
made by sun and wind
on the water of a pond
where I stood once
and gazed from a house no longer standing
with a woman no longer living,
both so clear to me now,
remembering light on the waves of Lake Michigan
where my seven-year-old feet
made tracks in the sand
toward water
where all tracks dissolve
till the stars return with sunlight and memory
as the breeze rises.

I

Weather comes up easily here in the mountains.
This day, darkening before noon
with ominous clouds, and then,
as if to mock them,
a shaft of sun comes through.

Setting off up the valley with no destination
other than this place from which I began,
I suppose it's finally the story of our lives,
an innocence nothing can equal.

Turning north to the edge of a hayfield,
skirting its border of scrub oak and pine—
leaving the mysterious forest unentered—
a dense sandwich of years, and my shoes kick up
echoes and dust.

2

God, is that you
tapping on my shutters this morning,
your redheaded herald,
the flicker,
opening small cracks
in the roof I've spent so much to maintain,
breaching the insulation of the phone lines
so the rains, now come,
make them bristle and pop,
your language my arrogance won't let me decipher?

■ ■ ■

How little we see even on the best days,
a few details,
broken grass stalks along the deer trail,
oaks swept eastward from the wind off the sea,
a few fragments of bone and feathers,
the intrigue of a life interrupted,
now that the hills have wrapped themselves in clouds.

■ ■ ■

Stars go on watching through this long afternoon
while I breathe in the sky and am still not filled.
The sun, a galaxy of blood through my eyelids;
wind now a river of smoke
through the long grass over the hills.

3

I am always returning to the edge of water,
lapping at the loam of a bank under pine needles,
and slapping at the bellies of dock planks.
Or I'm looking into one of those still, black ponds,
which seems to me like a pupil of the planet,
through which it watches the other stars
and finally our own silent faces,
gazing down to its ever-intensified heart.

■ ■ ■

Today an atutum wind
holds us a moment in stasis against the flow
as we squint through the rain toward a glint of sun
a mile downstream.

Three elk—cow, calf, and bull—
trot into the pines as we approach,
only to put a few boughs,
like another language, between us.

4

And what do the animals really know about our lives?
It seems they look on with unclouded ambition
to simply be more themselves
while we go on longing for their kind of grace.

Every night for three months, the fox
came to my bedroom window
and, in the wildness of her call,
I heard something so certain it stunned my heart
with what I once was, and may
yet be.

■ ■ ■

To stones on the riverbed
the current is a constant breeze,
the wind of Earth's turning
we can't feel anymore.

I lift my fly through moving air
for the joy of laying it down
in seams and eddies
where a fish might be.

In the last light the deer come closer;
their long shadows give them courage.

I press my dog's forehead to my own
and hold it till I feel her calmness seep through,
till the restless equation I've made of the world
is simply the world again.

Doing Nothing

When I passed him near the bus stop
on Union Square while the cops
cuffed his hands behind his back, while he
said, "I didn't *do* anything,"
I didn't, either,
do anything but look away,
a little afraid they might cuff me
if I paid too much attention,
and walked on still wondering
what he might've done
and still more what *I*
might've done.

Six Miles Up

The shadow of a hand brushes over the mountains,
as if smoothing rumpled sheets.
And now I see that the mountains are clouds.

In my dreams,
I search for what I won't remember in the morning,
but I do remember the searching.

In Venice I ate cuttlefish, steamed
in its own black ink,
and now it's coming out of my fingers.

Across the aisle in a window seat,
a man like me is
reading a book in which words appear,
tracing an indelible line
through invisible sky
while the pilot's skill keeps us flying.

A Small Dark Thing

A small dark thing darts across the room.
Or does it only dart across my eye?

The wake of a soul
probing toward the opposite shore?

We wonder who let the cat out when we
come home from work
to find her curled like smoke in the succulent grass.

Someone who knows more than I'm willing to tell
calls late at night
when I'm just between dreams.

Out Walking in Early November

Only late sunlight
spattered under the oaks
and now a pair of redtails,
so effortlessly over the next range of hills
I wonder if they are taking it all in up there,
as I imagine,
and if they need me
to make it beautiful.

A Theory of Wind

for Django

The oxygen that the trees
conceive out of sunlight
backs up in the branches of a single oak.

A still morning, dead calm,
a new day just beginning
to penetrate the fog.

Maybe a crow calls to remind you
you are listening,
that the silence itself is a kind of song.

And then one tiny leaf starts to quiver.

The leaf, moved by your attention,
gives a little wave
and happens to brush another leaf,

and together they make a voice.

This glad commotion spreads along the limb
till the tree can't contain itself
any more than you can keep from hearing it
or feeling its breath on your face.

You are absolved of all responsibility now,
as the whole tree takes up this song,

which leaps like flame to the oak next door,

while the startled pine tries to hush it
and only makes matters worse
from the standpoint of stillness.

If you get down close to the ground now you will hear
how the normally complacent grass
is also infected.

You've seen it fan out in great swoops,
like a blush on the face of the sea.

Madam Wei Remembers

aka Wei Wan ca.1050

How we both looked down
to where you disappeared inside me.
I lifted my head from the pillow to watch
that mysterious dark child come between us.

Candor Seeks Its Own Unforeseeable Occasions

HAYDEN CARRUTH

Tonight the sky is holding its breath.
A dove moans in the rain.
The moon is a thousand miles wide.
Maybe I'll get lucky and take the wrong road.

The Call

My dog watches me with unblinking eyes,
a look she can hold forever, it seems.
She wants me to know what she knows —
that the law of the universe demands it —
that behind her steady gaze
open all the fields we've longed to cover,
thickets waiting to snag our coats,
ticks poised to drop from the trees,
coyote turds we must piss on,
that the earth is deep with unknowable others
and the odors they've left to entice us —
    if only I could smell them —
might be the actual handkerchief *designedly dropped*
by that dark daughter of memory
I've been courting all morning.

Eclipse

Our shadow sweeps the Sea of Tranquillity
till we're only a small bruise on the moon's left temple.

WWII

His mother blowing smoke rings in his ear
to soothe the earaches that came back
so she would hold him in her arms
another night and smoke another Lucky Strike
and sing another lullaby or tell another story
of how nothing was either wrong or right
but thinking made it so, that the earaches kept coming back
because the bad thoughts wanted out and he was
hoarding them inside, stubborn like his father,
"And your grandfather, too," she added,
the way you toss things unintended
on the fire you built
to burn up what you didn't want.

Meanwhile the war news on the radio,
something about Saipan — one of those words
like Tarawa or later Bastogne that conjured
ruined trees in black and white — a palm
with only two fronds left or half a plane tree
like a signpost, pointing a way the highway didn't go,
accompanied by the breezy music of longing, *not
sitting under the apple tree or being home for Christmas,*
though not this year — and looking back, home
seemed a place he'd never really been because
now it was a place he couldn't go, longing for longing,
for what he saw finally as old sorrows
in the amber light of memory, but longing still
because it filled the cold and terrifying space he called
the present, and all the gaping presents
waiting to become.

The Rain Poured Down

My mother weeping
in the dark hallway, in the arms of a man,
not my father,
as I sat at the top of the stairs unnoticed —
my mother weeping and pleading
for what I didn't know and can still only imagine,
for things to be somehow other than they were —
not knowing what I would change,
for, or to, or why,
only that my mother was weeping
in the arms of a man not me,
and the rain brought down the winter sky
and hid me in the walls that looked on,
indifferent to my mother's weeping,
or mine,
in the rain that brought down the dark afternoon.

Then

When I was seven, or maybe eight, I rode with my mother out to a farm where something I was told we wouldn't speak of had happened. A man and woman, young, as I remember—though all adults were old to me then—met her in the yard of that unpainted house and received the gift of food she brought, a casserole with tuna, and bread she had baked to a golden, nutty brown. I remember that I was made to stay in the back of our black '47 Chevrolet, and remember all this because of a worm on the mohair carpet, a worm squashed and glistening on the floor, and that the hair of the perhaps young woman was curly, as if it had lately been in ringlets, and that her face was so pale and haunted that I loved her, loved at least the sadness of her life, and that the woman and the man—who had black hair, I remember—stood in the yard and watched as my mother backed the car in the dry autumn grass and said to me over her shoulder, with a look not unlike that of the woman who was watching, "Remember this, and how lucky you are," though I don't remember why, only the feeling, the wonder left—the rest lost to childhood—and the sad young woman, so pale I could smell her, like sleep or the must of old lilacs, still waving after the man turned away, and the unlucky worm, green and still glistening, as the shadows of trees swept the floor and the Chevrolet whined away through its gears.

On Being Sent Away to School

When they called me to the office to tell me my grandfather
was dead, when Herbie Schellenberger, ex-corporal of the Third
Reich, who seemed old to a classroom of twelve-year-old boys
and told us, with ill-suppressed laughter, how funny things were
in the war, how his lieutenant, having failed in his duty at Bas-
togne, put the water-filled barrel of a Luger in his mouth and
how silly he looked with his head reduced to the size of a sauce-
pan, ridiculed the sentimentality of my missing so much Latin
because an old man was dead, how that first poem, "The High-
wayman" by Alfred Noyes, was my ticket to a light less harsh
where a beautiful woman gave her life for love, and how a mist
I might not have otherwise seen rose from the frost on the grass
as the sun beat down through the late autumn morning while I
lugged my suitcase out to catch the bus that would take me on
that long ride back to where a month ago I was a child.

The Day I Fled My Twelve-Year-Old Life

A river broadly flowing:
crossed to an island in a rented boat
— green oars, green boat, green
kingdom where I found,
for that one day, and years beyond,
another boy who could be me.

He had an easier way about him,
not smarting from the sting of school,
not lonely, though he lived alone,
not pining for his mother far away.
He rustled in the trees all afternoon
and purled in the current as it
hugged the island and moved on.

His spirits were snakes and birds and frogs.
His voice was in the breeze.
He told me I could come again,
that he'd be there, or anywhere,
if I would be there, too. If I
would just remember him,
the river, the boat, the bees,
and how the water
dazzled-back the sunlight
through the trees.

Sail Baby Sail

Now I sing to my mother, the lullabies she sang to me as a child. Her hand trembles to her mouth, as if to find the lips that once formed words, as if to move them again with her fingers into speech. She makes a face at me, and bounces her eyebrows as she would when she sang, *Gunk, gunk went the little bull froggy*, and I smooth back her hair as I sing to her now, *Gunk, gunk went the lady froggy, too.* She laughs, and for a moment her trembling is gone. She holds her smile like a note sustained at the end of a phrase, like a child waiting for another surprise. I tickle her forehead, and remember a twilight over her shoulder, or think I remember, and the creaking of the chair as we rocked and the perfume she wore. *Sail baby, sail,* I half mumble, half sing, *far across the sea. Only don't forget to sail, home again to me.* She cries, and I catch her tears in a tissue, my "tear catcher," I call it, and she laughs. Something is passing between us, something I felt a dozen years ago as I talked to my father long after he'd stopped breathing, something that holds us together, something like music, something we might carry to another life, like the sound of a human voice talking.

Dorothy

*How can that depth be fathomed where a man may see
himself reflected?*

THOREAU

I held her hand through her last drugged sleep
and called the names that used to make her smile
    Mother, Mom,
names I'd pled with as a child
to let me be with her.

Dorothy Marion Scott, she insisted
as her illness worked its course,
never married, never gave birth,
still asking for her parents,
as if they'd suddenly been called away
or simply wandered off
to view some paintings in a church
far away.

My words were only sounds now, coming back,
just slight rhyme and assonance,
until I said, "Dorothy,"
the name I'd never called before.

Her eyes opened.
I saw myself there twice.
I wonder who she was just then,
and whether she saw me gazing in
before they closed again.

Lying under the Oaks on a Morning in June

I can't tell now whether I'm drifting
among the roots or the branches,
rising into the clear spring sky
or drawn down to lie
with those dear, departed selves
I loved and couldn't help
but go on loving.

Six Kinds of Gratitude

1

I'm someone's small boat,
far out at sea,
sailing from what has so long sustained me
toward what I don't know.

My joy is the sound
of the water purling around me,
but is it my hull
or the great ocean moving?

2

Are those flies I hear, or a trick of the wind,
faintly human voices,
or a whistle of breath
in the nose of my sleeping dog?

3

Without *me* there is no confusion.
Buddhas see no difference between
themselves and others; Angels,
between the living and the dead.

4

At last I've discovered
the secret of life:
*If you don't leave
you can't come back.*

5

Deep in the earth there are pockets of light
that did not come from heaven,
and yet they are the light of heaven
deep inside the earth.

6

This bird is the birdness of a bird.

Facing North

Ninety billion galaxies in this one tiny universe —
a billion seconds make thirty-four years.

No matter how many ways we conceive it,
this generous wedge called Ursa Major
more than fills my sight.

But now, as I turn to put out the lights
and give my dog her bedtime cookie,
my eyes become the handle of the great Milky Way,
and carry it into the house.

Five Poems: Off the Beaten Track

I

Deep in the mountains;
few friends come to see us.

At times we experience the past as an avalanche,
at others as an anchor,
till our raft is swept
beyond the sight of land
on water we haven't yet seen.

2

My dog barks,
announcing the arrival of Tuesday.

She watches its light lumber through the oaks
as it creeps up the hill from the sea.

Life is always three or four things
occurring to me all at one time.

3

I want to preserve this dawn —
a small stone we can suck on.

Everything flies away, and a photograph
is only a photograph, especially
of something so beautiful.

4

Without even trying
this white pebble radiates
tiny white rings with a vitreous humor,

a moon leaving Saturn
in the nick of time.

5

White cattle wend their way
along the canyon road.

Saints in procession under the oaks.

2004

When your country has been a bad citizen again
and you're a little ashamed of her,
as you were of your four-year-old
when she threw another tantrum at the mall,
and you wanted to pretend you didn't know her,
that you weren't responsible for her bad behavior,
a citizen of the world, as you wish she would be.

Still her mountains glow in the late evening sun,
and your neighbors, who voted to support her arrogance,
smile kindly when you greet them, and you're moved,
observing their obvious affection for each other,
how he pulls up her collar against the chill breeze
and she smooths back his comb-over again and again.

You saw this in Cincinnati and again in Darfur,
people being conscious and considerate of others,
and you wonder how we ever draw the line
about whom we choose to comfort and whom
it might be quite permissible to kill.

Heroes

The Grail is being in perfect accord with the abundance of nature.

JOSEPH CAMPBELL

The path Buddha took away from the world
was the path he took coming back,
but when Ulysses returned home from Troy
he came a much longer way.

Falling into habits you become a target;
whoever wants to may do you great harm,
though being a target may be who you are.

Suppose Jesus kissed Judas and snuck out of the garden,
or the Buddha returned to his palace as a beggar
and slew all the louts who took up with his wife,
or Ulysses sailed back in sunlight,
a gentle old man now, anointed in blood,
and forgave those who trespassed against him,

or that Parzival found the abiding Grail—
that question killed by an answer—
and sold it.

A Primer on Parallel Lives

Bees and sprinklers employ the silence,
and a horse screaming over the hill.

According to Euclid, Hades has no depth,
no echoes, no valleys, no heart's embrace.

Now the faintest curve of a sycamore
begins to shine through the fog,

and the window we look out of
becomes the frame in which we're displayed.

At Any Moment

This anger sneaks back in
like the thought of a white horse
I'm determined to ignore,
my heart on fire with intolerance
of intolerance,
the wars I fight against the wars
in me. I have come to regret
being right about anything.

Contemplating My Reflection in a Puddle on the Last Day of the Twentieth Century

Even this still water wants to be somewhere else,
another way of saying it's motion
seeking space,
drawn to the earth as rain,
or into the air as vapor,
off on a quest, in-
eluctably drawn to find itself,
disguised in you and me.

To Study the Way

My world this morning made simple
by the fog out my window,
this one tree, and beyond it
no distant mountains
through the large, open windows of the oak,
no pale grass hillside, or horses,
no deer standing stark still, listening
for any movement, looking
back my way for some slight
sign I may be watching,
whatever I may be.

After the Rain

I spot a young barn owl
standing by the road
peering at his own reflection in a puddle,
or so it seems,
when I pull onto the shoulder to see
if I can help.

Dazed,
probably struck by a car,
though not visibly wounded,
he looks up across the puddle
where I'm standing,
as if to ask about this
wondrous, underground bird he is seeing,
as if to ask if I see it, too.

Some Distance

I wanted to be a stone in the field,
simply that,
and then I wanted to be the grass around it,
and then the cattle grazing
under the too blue sky,
and then the blue,
which has of itself
no substance,
and yet goes on and on and on.

from SAILING THROUGH CASSIOPEIA

2012

The inner—what is it?
if not intensified sky,
hurled through with birds and deep
with the winds of homecoming.

RILKE

In Our Rented Cabin

I live my late years as if I've stolen my life.
TU FU 712–770

My son and grandson sleep in the next room.
I've been awake and up for hours,
and they will likely sleep a few more.

Is it an old man's hunger
to take in all he can
of what's left of his life?

Though still a year short of seventy,
not really old, yet
my father and grandfather didn't
live much past it.

This morning I think I'm up early for them,
watching the first light
spread like soft butter
over the rolling meadows of the foothills
and the little green pastures
on the mountains above.

I can't get enough of this moment.

What is it that urges me on
to take it all in,
to save what I can
for them to see through my eyes?

Barking and Howling

The coyotes
shadow us all morning
from the slopes above the valley.
I call to my dogs to try
to bring them in close,
their hearing already more than half-
consumed by the taunts of these
ancient cousins,
like prideful Fetterman and his callow troops,
lured to their deaths over Lodge Trail Ridge
by Crazy Horse on his spotted mare.

■ ■ ■

Yesterday I saw a coyote
standing by the road.
I stopped and looked at her,
and she looked back at me.
She didn't appear threatened,
or threatening, or nervous,
or displaced, or displeased,
or wanton, or hungry,
or curious, or annoyed,
or anything at all.
She just looked at me while
I stood and looked at her.
And then she turned
and trotted off into the morning.

■ ■ ■

The coyotes in the canyon
are making a kill.

Their voices
rise through the darkness,
a chorus of hundreds it seems,
most likely closing in
on the spotted fawn I saw this morning,
dragging its right hind leg
to keep up with its mother and twin.

I pray it may not be
the wounded fawn I saw,
now trembling in fear.

Another perhaps
but not that one.

Crocus

Thirty-six years ago my father died
while snow was melting
and white and yellow crocuses,
in their spiked cups of bright green,
　　push their way into the air,
through soil that's just now waking up.

Without even noticing,
I'm in the present tense.

Does this mean the soil
is just now waking up,
though, by the calendar, it's the 12th of July?

Or does it mean
we're always in the present,
wherever we may be thinking?

And where will I find a crocus
in the withering heat of mid-July? —
fragile, teasing, iridaceous
little flower
I otherwise hardly ever think of.

from Roses in the Cool Café

> *The rose laughs at my long-looking,*
> *my constantly wondering what*
> *a* rose *means, and who* owns
> *the rose, whatever it means.*
>
> RUMI

3

Does your life end when we sever your stem
and interrupt your affair with the soil?
Or do you continue for a while—
cooling in the adoration of our gaze—
to sense our presence
and possibly even the caress of the air
we breathe out
after taking in all we can
of your barely traceable scent?

I see how you still seem to flourish
and sometimes for several days go on opening,
before the age in your petals
draws back the delight
that kept you so fresh in our eyes.

Call Me

Suddenly, for reasons no one can
explain or understand,
I can't read anymore.
English on the page looks like
Turkish to me.
Did I just forget?
It feels like I never knew how.

I can still write though.
I can think these words to the page—
just for you—
but don't know if they make any sense.

Here's my phone number—
which I can remember.

When you come across this puzzle
please call.

Please call and let me know who I am.

Under the Pines

Every day another alarm.
No more ice at the pole, no more
fish in the sea,
the pollen-bearing bees
bearing off to the moon.

No more love, will they tell me
no more love?

Suddenly the boughs fill with wind and quiet
the world as it is just now.

Groundhog Day

for Emmylou

I hear a muffled yelp from the hallway.
Our old dog, Eudora, has made a wrong move
and tweaked the crumbling disks in her spine.

Otherwise she's happy I think.
She pants and thumps her indefatigable
tail against my leg

when we pause on our gentle walk
over the hills and still
defers to her nose above all other callings.

I don't think she knows she will die.
I don't think she suffers concern
over what she may have to endure

tomorrow or the day after or that
a month from now she may lose me
or the woman we live with who

reads the look in her eyes and speaks
for her in a language only the tone
of which she understands. And it's enough

that she smells coyotes and truck tires and
the soon-to-be-dead, equally
without regret,

like this curly brown feather
just fallen
from a bird we didn't see.

Refuge

I watched the sunset on Mars
through a space-probe camera's eye.

It dropped down so quickly—
like a diver in a slow-motion film

plunging into darkness
through a last splash of light.

I heard soft knocking
at my door.

Then an acorn struck
and rolled forever down the roof.

A crow cawed faintly
beyond the closed window.

Autumn, and the fire
flaps like heavy canvas in the wind.

Postscript

I think I may have startled you,
signing this letter
with *love* at the end,
that you may think
I'm being too familiar,
sending the wrong signal,
that we don't know each other
that well,
that there's so much about you
I'd find unlovable
if I *really*
knew the real you,
that I've overstepped,
invaded your space,
that I may want you
to love me, that this
could complicate our lives
impossibly,
that…

among people,
I think of my father
telling me an hour
before he died,
how he thought of all the
men and women he'd loved
and how
he wished he'd told them
when he could've.

Dyslexic

When I was in the second grade,
and they didn't yet have the word,
my parents hired a special teacher
to help me get by with my spelling.

After a week of frustration,
my teacher quit.

It was like trying to reeducate a magnet,
he told my mother. As if
I'd been born into the wrong language, he said.

Polio

In the second week of September, a few weeks past my ninth birthday, I began to feel the ache in my arms and legs, as if the giant who had chased me through the sand dunes the previous summer were squeezing my tiny thighs and biceps with his many huge hands, like dough being kneaded into breadsticks, while Mrs. Borman, standing by the leathery, pastel-shaded, pull-down map of South America, explained the independence of a continent and how heat builds up along the equator — where the sun never takes a vacation — and I felt the heat building up in my forehead as I reached down from my desk to pick up the pencil, just fallen from my fingers, the weight of it pulling me, in slow-motion, like a tree sloth, to a stratum below the nervous laughter of my classmates and Mrs. Borman's scolding voice, as the giant began tightening the drawstring of the black bag into which the school principal's face intruded, and then my big sister Scotti's, and I was being carried out to a car in a bag so dark now I couldn't remember where its mouth had been or the fourth grade, or September, or my best friend Art, or my Schwinn two-wheeler, only the oracular faces in the darkness touting a destiny as remote as Oz — *Danny, you're going to be okay. You're going to come through this Danny. You will* — the ablative voices coaxing me from my fear of becoming a huge, huffing cylinder with a tiny head sticking out, the faces appearing and fading in an endless hot night, a radio whistling, trombones moaning, the voice of Vaughn Monroe singing "Ghost Riders in the Sky," my mother singing lullabies, my nurse, soothing my forehead with cold, wet rags, and months later my father, having asked whether there was anything in the world I wanted, bringing the new Rawlings catcher's mitt, taking it from the box, laying it on the bedcovers and lifting my sleeping hand up to rest on it.

Advice

You know how, after it rains,
my father told me one August afternoon
when I struggled with something
hurtful my best friend had said,
how worms come out and
crawl all over the sidewalk
and it stays a big mess
a long time after it's over
if you step on them?

Leave them alone,
he went on to say,
after clearing his throat,
and when the rain stops,
they crawl back into the ground.

Anna Karenina

Because my mother was consumed with longing
for music and dance,
the passions of Lawrence,
the imagined life of Deauville
and the Côte d'Azur,
for the dark, chaotic prince who
ransomed her heart,

my father lived out his life alone
in that rambling house they shared —
two vast, yearning,
proximate stars,
caught up in separate constellations.

Old Dog

She has lived in us like rain in clouds,
and now, unsteady on her feet,
half deaf, half blind, half daft,
her nights a futile thrashing
to find a posture for sleep,
while she pants in near exhaustion.

She loves to be scratched
behind the ears her paws
can no longer reach
while she stands huffing and swaying
with grateful eyes.

I doubt she feels the sense of doom
we carry
in our also-aging bodies.

Maybe our job
is to feel that for her.
Maybe hers is to show us how.

To God Himself in the Passing Hours

Through the boy who is me at the moment,
quite out of his mind,
wed to his shadow on the grass
as he twirls to keep it twirling,

and the clatter of the mower whirling
through a still, spring morning —
the bleating of the stems that
cling to the blades —
a kind of preaching we seldom
hear anymore,

I bow to the life being lived in this finch
and to the one I found, rock-still,
below the window on my terrace
this morning,

and to the pale moon now,
askew in the sky. I
can't imagine it
further adrift.

On My Seventieth Birthday

Let everything happen to you:
beauty and terror.
Only press on: no feeling is final.

RILKE

Tens of thousands of people
have drowned in Bangladesh
and a million more
may die from isolation, hunger, cholera,
and its sisters, thirst and loneliness.

■ ■ ■

This morning, in our lime tree,
I noticed a bee
dusting a single new bud,
just now beginning to bloom,
while all the other branches were sagging
with heavy green fruit.

■ ■ ■

I read that in Moscow
every man, woman, child, and dog
is inhaling eight packs of cigarettes a day —
or its equivalent in smoke —
from the fires raging over the steppes.

■ ■ ■

The god of storms
took the shape of a tree,

bowing to the desert
with her back to the sea.

I saw, on television,
a woman in Iran buried up to her breasts,
then wrapped in light gauze
(to protect the spectators),
weeping in terror and pleading for her life
while someone at the edge of the circle
of men dressed in black
picked up the first baseball-sized rock
from the hayrick-sized pile,
to hurl at her eyes, nose, mouth,
ears, throat, breasts, and shoulders.

■ ■ ■

How big is my heart, I wonder.
How will it encompass these men dressed in black?

■ ■ ■

Now the fog drifts in over the passes,
screening the peaks into halftones.
And then into no tones at all.

■ ■ ■

These goats with names,
with eyes that make you wonder,
these goats
who will be slaughtered today.
Why *these* goats?

■ ■ ■

There are reasons,
but they are human reasons.

■ ■ ■

I listened while my friend
spoke through his grief for his son,
shot to death in the pizza shop he managed
in Nashville
after emptying the safe
for a desperate young man with a gun —
    who my friend told me he'd forgiven —
spoke of consolation through his tears,
the spirit of his son still with him, he said.
The spirit of his son still with him.

■ ■ ■

Oak tree,
joy of my eye
that reaches in so many directions —
are the birds that fly from your branches
any closer to heaven?

■ ■ ■

The moon
shimmering on the surface of the pond,
its rippling reflected in your eyes,
of which you are no more aware
than the wind, just passing through this oak,
of the acorns still bobbing.

■ ■ ■

The mountains, resolute now
in fading light.
With her nose deep in the late-summer grass,
my dog calls up a new story.

Nostalgia

The moon is always full;
our point of view has its phases.

I return to houses that no longer exist, a form
of self-immolation that, mixed with time, can be fatal.

Knowledge seeks an empty cup.
So does desire.

We are drawn to the past
because we think it knows its future.

Half-withered tree
that delights this day in seeing me.

The necessity of a necessity
finding its form.

In these branches, a god who never was
until she had a home.

Your death, that speck adrift in your eye.
Don't hesitate to seek its advice.

Even the dust has its dust.

Often I Imagine the Earth

Often I imagine the earth
through the eyes of the atoms we're made of—
atoms, peculiar
atoms everywhere—
no me, no you, no opinions,
no beginning, no middle, no end,
soaring together like those
ancient Chinese birds
hatched miraculously with only one wing,
helping each other fly home.

Snail

Nothing ever leaves this universe.
It is but transformed, said Ovid.

Sometimes too much meaning,
real meaning, deep meaning...

As the fog lifts, the landscape
loses its philosophy.

The man who draws the shell precisely
is content,

while the poet circles to begin, he hopes,
to experience its intimate shellness.

What's more abstract than this
borrowed house we're wearing?

Did you fail to recognize the gift
because it required... everything?

Tiny eremite at play in the grass
where God is proclaiming the present.

Wang Wei in His Leisure Hours

He somehow cobbled together his career as a renowned hermit in whatever free time his office job allowed.

DAVID HINTON

This tiny gentian,
so faithful to the earth in its teardrop
of honey-colored amber, bloomed
and became immortal
thirty-five million years before
anyone thought of God.

And today I read that we exist
because of a cosmic imbalance.
For a reason no one understands, the universe
contains just a little more
matter than antimatter.

Wang sought an image of a world
that fled like darkness from his lamp.

He found himself in the trees,
the grass and leaves, the river,
the fawn come to drink in
the landscape of midsummer.

Verlaine called the universe a flaw
in the purity of nonexistence;
Keats, "the vale of soul-making."
Rilke said,
"I have such pure mornings,"
and Cavafy lamented

that night returns to draw us back
with its "same fatal pleasure."

Wang wondered why the spring breeze
blew its scattered blossoms to his door.

Above the mountain, the day's
first cloud turns from
gray, to mauve, to gold.

He found springtime
in a pot of wine, which
often brought with it a poem,
often carried it away
before he could write it down.

Art

If I found the body of a dragonfly
I'd keep it, at least for a while,

to keep in mind the impossible beauty
of the mind taking flight,

the fluid geometry
of the heart settling.

Mahler labors up out of a dark pond
to work his wings, preparing.

A tree in the palm of my hand sways.
A bird in its branches sings.

A million atoms, like arrows,
mad to find a target in the mind.

"The dark is always at the top"

MARK ROTHKO

1

While I waited for the waitress
to bring my iced tea,
a fly, clinging to the body
of the saltshaker, let go,
suddenly dropped to the table
on its back, kicked
two or three of its legs in the air,
and died.

2

Every day we bear up under
the liminal weight of air,
a million pounds and more,
in tiny increments
because we've grown used to it,
like the heat of our own blood
we remark only in a fever
or in the bodies of others.

3

How did Jesus picture the cup
he asked the Father to take from him,
and what did Saint Teresa have in mind
when she prayed to be released
from the consolations of the world?

4

Sunflower,
heavy-headed girl
gazing down on me,
surrounding world
that will not be denied,
heart that longs to fly with
everything it loves,
let go.

To a Tick

I feel your devotion,
though it doesn't feel
quite like love.

I've literally got you,
who dropped in
uninvited, under my skin,
as the old song goes, you
of whom I was even unaware
till I became inflamed
with your presence
and you engorged with mine.

What a perfect couple we are
now, living off the same blood.

Dusk

The stag,
leaping across the November highway,

broke clean in two
between ribs, at the withers,

steam rising into the cold evening air
above its still-pulsing heart.

The man with the bloody face,
behind the caved-in windshield of the van,

asks, "What should I do?"
Asks it twice.

"Can I keep the deer?"
asks the kid from the Camaro,

pulled up on the shoulder
behind the van.

"Don't move," I said.
"Just don't move."

The deer's heart throbbed
one more time.

The deer's heart,
in the first clear light of its life,
stopped beating.

Sailing through Cassiopeia

The sky is round because the eye is round.
A high soprano singing from the fire.

Serpentine hieroglyphics of worm tracks
through the oak.

The clear lubricious wine
that seeps from her most secret space.

Her eyes telling me it's time to come inside.
Moments of ecstasy on the lip of terror.

The tightrope walker lives by continuance;
the trapeze artist by letting go.

I dream I'm dreaming I wake up
still dreaming.

Learning to say *avoirdupois*
and never saying it again.

The crow and the quail sang a duet in the fog —
though never quite ever together.

We miss our dead friends because we've lost our last chance
to make them change their minds.

My conclusions end in question marks.

Say *home entertainment* eighteen times,
real fast.

Passing the window, he glances over,
hoping his reflection won't glance back.

"I grow hoarse," said Horace.
"I must have been seen by a wolf."

Matsu kazi.
Trying to photograph the wind in the pines.

How could a woman with such a teeny-weenie voice
have such a beautiful big butt?

The little town along the river wasn't my town
but the next town down Route 32.

The half-finished houses still waiting.

When I'm gone will there still be the spring wind,
and still my walking in it?

You are not someone else;
someone else is.

When one becomes two,
there's always one more in between.

The falling shadows of afternoon light.
The mountains flexing their muscles.

Ice can't freeze and water
can't melt.

I saw a bird in the fire
where no bird can be.

Pictures of nothing I've seen.
Pictures the mind makes beautiful.

Because you were awake
a single star broke its moorings.

Climbing two hours this morning with my dogs
and still no certain glimpses of the sea.

In my dream I had no reflection.
When I woke I saw through the mirror.

The newly reincarnated mayflies.
Bright fluttering stars above the river.

The silent greeting from a satellite
sailing through Cassiopeia.

NEW POEMS

A Few Words

If there are words that would
rescue the earth
from other words
that would destroy her,
I'd want to speak them
as purely as the grass
turns green on the heels
of a late-winter storm.

I don't know what they would be
or whether such words could exist.
Earth herself remains silent
in her steady course past the sun,
so I listen, and watch,
and even guess
sometimes, writing them down,
hoping someone
may find and refine them,
urging her on through her seasons.

Spring Suite

I: RAIN

It was only the wind
as it began, not quite even

wind yet, just a bobbing
of the outer branches,

by which we could see it
moving toward us —

the sudden exhalation of
ozone flooding our faces

as the air cooled
around our arms —

we looked
for tiny specks

on the dry stones and
found them.

2: RED-STEMMED FILAREE

Though no one
seems to know its name,

it's everywhere
after the rains, casting

the hillsides in its almost
ultra-violet hue —

a half-million tiny
bursts. They seem

the fallen diorama
of a moonless

night under which
all our questions blink out.

3: COLD FRONT

The wind rose midmorning
from a quickening

breeze to a guttural
stammer, as if trying

for a song it could never
get right, and remained

angry past sunset,
tearing at the shingles —

scattering poppies and
fiesta flowers

in their first attempts at beauty.

Awake

I thought I heard someone at the door,
but it was only the sun
still behind the mountain
and three deer nibbling
the frosty grass of September.

■ ■ ■

Incense smoke bends a beautiful arc
across the ceiling in the first morning light,
expounding its dharma to my eyes,
a barred cloud, a wisp,
the memory of a dream.

■ ■ ■

Out the window, a jaguar,
muscular and coated with spots like
bright golden eyes,
sleeping in the garden,
or pretending to sleep,
though I also saw *his* dream
sleeping in the garden above him.

Pigeons

Every ten or fifteen minutes, like a wave
no longer able to hold itself in, the pigeons
explode from the live oak with a
whump and clatter that will
startle if you're close by,
83 of them by my approximate count
fan out over the canyon
and circle back
as if seeking the unseen
face of what scared them away,
a winged shadow streaking
the grassy verge of the field,
a bobcat padding through leafless chaparral,
me stepping out into the yard

or possibly the tree itself—
reaching its tolerance for pigeon-commotion—
simply shrugs them off
in the silent, molecular way of trees,
giving its trunk a cellular shiver

or maybe something in their pigeon-genes
makes this company
one too many pigeons to bear,
that 82nd other
that breaks the tension at the brim
of the glass already too full.

They return in twos, and threes, and fours,
silhouettes of wing-sets gliding

back into their diffuse labyrinth
of thicket, threat, leaves,
and fragments of sky
with a rustle and resettling of wings.

The Work of the Bees

Barry Spacks 1931–2014

Barry died at 6:30 p.m.
the last Tuesday in January—his heart
living on an hour longer than the sun
that day.

Earth is the only place that knows
suffering and little blue flowers
showing their throats to the sky.

The bees were busy in the gardens
everywhere, and
then they were gone.

In China,
a great nostalgia for honey.

A million young men
and a million
women on ladders in the orchards with
fine-haired brushes in their hands,
painting tiny stigmas in the
kingdoms of the anther—
doing the work of the bees.

Only on Earth, where grief is.

With nothing to attain, the awakened
being depends on the wisdom of having
already crossed over—already looking back
from the other shore.

More and More

Do the crickets sing
in the tall, autumn grass,
or only in the labyrinth
of the ear?

I hear them
under the glittering stars
and again when I close the door
in the otherwise still, silent house.

I've read that the bees are going
away. No one knows where,
only that more and more,
they fail to return.

I hear them in the lavender
and Mexican sage
and skirt them with caution,

savoring the *subtle electric*
thrill of their buzz
and my own small fear
of being stung.

To Pain

You begin the moment I wake up,
and even the moment before,
abiding companion, herald of my life,
though a little too strident at times.

I have little white pills to calm,
and even still, you. Sometimes
I think you've finally walked out,
but a little neglect is all it takes to win you back.

When you've stayed too long, I might
demand to know why you've chosen *me*.
What I may have done to summon you.
What retribution you represent.

But you tell me nothing more,
only that you are part of what a body feels,
only that you're part of what a heart endures
and what a mind transforms.

You are, after all,
like the fog this morning,
obscuring almost everything, till a tree emerges just beyond
        our yard,

and then, again, a fence corner
coming almost imperceptibly
back into view,
halfway up the next hill.

Climate

In this heat and marathon drought
the seasons have gotten confused.

Two tarantulas crossing the road this
morning, looking for love as they do

this time of year, although we're
actually just into the fall, while

the struggling young oak in the yard,
which normally breaks its buds in

February when it's normally raining,
brought out its new leaves just a

month ago in early September.
How can this be, and

what will the tree do
now when winter arrives?

Bliss

I have eaten the first fruit of the season,
and I am in love.

JAMES WRIGHT

The large, spotted donkey
billows up her great bag of wind
to bray for the cookies in my pockets
and the attention she craves
from my still half-sleeping mind.

She lifts her chin to the lip
of her stall's half door,
so I bend to lower mine.

Nose pressed to nose,
we exchange warm breaths,
hers of clover, timothy, and sweetgrass,
mine sour with strong coffee
and last night's bitter words.

She has no sense of early or late.
She has no sense of tomorrow.

I take in another of her mesmerizing breaths,
like a hive-bee receiving
half-distilled honey
from the worker who just brought it home,
half infected by the sweetness
of its having been hers.

Pebble

Love is finally the desire to create
the thing loved, said Valéry. Beauty

the embodied energy we attend to.
A pebble falling through

a clear stream on a planet falling
toward a star falling into the Milky Way.

Nonzero equals not equal to zero in any
description of life. In our headlights

last night Deb saw a rabbit and I saw
a fox — both of us certain what we'd seen.

Foreign

The once elegant facade of the
hotel in Caracas bore
the ravaged expression of a leper,
face of the moon, pocked
with the craters of
three dozen .50-caliber
bursts of a *machina* from the most
recent attempt at a revolution.

Inside, it was an ordinary,
dark hotel, pretending
to its everyday pathos. "Sorry
for any inconvenience."
The concierge replied
to my inquiry in English.
"Reparations
have already been planned."

Dust II

How the dust scattered on the shiny, black cover
of the book on my footstool in the

first morning light through the window
resembles the moonless sky

I sat out under — amazed
by my inability to grasp it —

that both of us — the universe
and I — could be so close and so

impossibly distant — that I can
so easily touch the stars with my eyes

and be so consummately nothing
without them — how I could

clear the black field of the book
with one swipe of my hand and how

I could, also, decide not to.

Dark Matter

The visible drapes itself around the invisible,
the way the jacket takes its shape from the shoulders.

An unseen gravity whirls
near the center of our galaxy,

an unseen heart near the center
of the bodies in which we desire.

I seldom think of Neptune out there, way beyond
pointing to it on a summer night.

Would twenty-five trillion miles impress you —
the distance to our next nearest sun?

Would seventy million degrees Fahrenheit —
the temperature at its core?

I sit up under the late-August stars,
at ease in their assurance and grace,

happy to incomprehend them,

to be the dark in the darkness
and the light in the spaces between.

The Turkey Vulture

The vulture sidled up
to the tin chicken on the garden wall,
and — showing off —
stretched out his scarlet neck
as if to scrutinize
some aspect of the day,
then spread hunched wings
and let them hang to dry.

How I love this grotesque
lord of the air,
come down out of his soaring —
as we all must —
to humor the everyday
lust of our lives.

Fire Season

John Branquinho has set up his steel
fence panels around the concrete
waterers, preparing to recapture
the cattle he released last fall
after the first rains turned
the brown hills green again.

The cows crop the grass and weeds
down close so there's less to catch fire
now it's all dried out, and they
watch us with slow, only slightly curious eyes
as we pass. Sometimes they
tag along a little way down the road.

A winter of freedom —
nooning-up under the oaks —
so placid and self-contained —
mounting each other with oblique affection,
stretching their necks as high as they can
to pull down the low-hanging browse.

I begin to miss them already
on these morning walks with the dogs
and wish them some seamless way
out of this life,
without pain or fear wherever
the big trucks take them tomorrow.

Letter to Jim about Woodpeckers

The woodpeckers are knocking on the house again.
I could waste the whole day
rushing out the door to scare them away,
but as soon as I return to this letter
they're back to remind us that everything
changes — every millisecond — constantly.

I've been reading a dense book on
our best guess about what might have
happened in the first three seconds
of existence — a fraction
of the time it's taken me to write this line
in which the cause of everything

leading up to our consciousness of it
was set and wonder whether that alone could be
why anything at all exists —
so that for only a brief flashing of
beauty and terror we might see it and wonder
about abiding things like woodpeckers and
the dogged opinions of people we love.

Waiting for My Father to Speak

My father gone now, forty years,
longer ago than I'd been alive

when I sat by his bed
and watched him drift away,

half-expecting to hear him
clear his throat once more,

as he always would at the end
of an interminable half-minute

pause in midsentence — waiting
with all the time in the world

for just the right word to occur —
while I sat enduring my heartbeat

and breath, silently, madly,
urging him on as *I* always had,

both of us still waiting
for the perfect word.

Infinite in All Directions

The disappearing moon
accepting, as she does, her sentence of dark
has *nothing* to say in the sun's patient dance
with the shadow of the earth —
still falling.

■ ■ ■

But *nothing* is always something
waiting, like light, for the mind
to catch up with the billion
galaxies we can see out there,
glowing like clusters of madrepore,
through our great wandering, magnified eyes,
or, turning our self-forgetful
attention inside,
to the ever-expanding in-
finitesimal.

Second Look

The cougar moves at ease
around our house: soft
tracks between the lilacs
below our bedroom window and
one smudged print of soil on the sill
where she must have braced her paw
to look in.

I saw her only once,
on a rise of the deer-trail
a stone's throw ahead, looking
back at me over her shoulder.

She brandished her tail three times
in warning, like a sword, as if
to say, *I'm here where I
have always been*, then shat
to put a period on it and
sauntered on over the hill.

■ ■ ■

I praise the animals that abide
generation after human
generation, the same
bird call that stopped
my great grandfather one spring
evening in his yard,
spring peepers again, affirming
the first-appearing stars at dusk,

how faint the meanings,
how bright the sound. Now, in
fading light, the earth closer again
as when I was the sky,
a child looking into everything,
hardly sensing anyone looking.

Voyage

*The ship, slow and rushing at the same time, can get ahead of
the water
but not the sky.*

JIMÉNEZ

Can you remember,
Juan Ramón,
the name of the I
still standing unseen beside you,

the name of the boat
stuck in the shadow
of the depths below
and the latitude of the small waves lapping,

the name of the god
for whom you built a refuge,
from your hope and the flame
drawn back to the coal?

Was the god's name *Awake*,
to the day that is only today,
the sea roads laid out in delight,
trailing silver behind you?

Nirvana

A hundred quail on the grass outside my window,
and the dogs are a little upset,
and at least one hundred doves —
band-tailed pigeons — in the tree above,
and one crow complaining for all he's worth
about the world as it is right now.

■ ■ ■

I had a conversation with a coyote
ambling along the road at dusk,
while I was driving home last night.
I rolled down the window
and asked what kind of a day he'd had,
and he just shrugged.
Or I thought he shrugged.

■ ■ ■

Later, as I walked
near a thicket of brooding young oaks,
a startled owl flew up
through the paler darkness of moonlight,
and the trailing feathers
of one of its wings
brushed my busy life into silence.

The Weather Channel

Men standing out in storms,
talking,
telling us how violent the wind is,
showing us they can still stand up to it,
though just barely,
telling us that *we* should stay inside,
that to do otherwise would be foolish,
we at home who are not experienced storm-standers.

Secretly,
we want to see this grizzled lover of Chaos
take flight —
not lost forever, of course —
batted around just rudely enough
to be convinced of his own advice.

This World Too

The allure of the anther
waiting for the bee's embrace.

A sudden silence when I see the dragonfly,
my lips sewn shut with wonder.

The magic is in the pains
the magician takes to deceive you.

The sky lightened for a moment,
but there was only the gravel shoulder

of the road on my left
where I thought a shadow might be.

Every time I begin to write, something
touches my hand, says *No, not yet.*

Lusting after is judging too;
a leaf I first took for a stone.

Spring Creek

Standing at ease in the current,
watching my thoughts stream by,
seventeen thousand thoughts in a day.
If I grasp one the river stops flowing.

Those horses on the walls of the Chauvet cave,
twenty thousand years before the pharaohs —
unsurpassed and thoroughly modern —
before Homer, Heraclitus, or Pollock.

Do we think of pigeons as lowly
because they crowd our trees and the empty spring sky?
I saw one torn apart by a hawk — one bird —
and at that moment I grieved.

My grief is here with my joy now,
wingtip to talon, they circle,
one closer at first, then the other.

Summers with Martha

I spent those dream-like summers with Martha
in a cottage on Lake Michigan,
the year Ike beat Taft and the awful
summer they killed the Rosenbergs.
Martha smoked her Chesterfields
and knitted through nights of crickets
and whispers along the shore.

She appeared and vanished
according to my mother's curious compass reading
of where my affections might lie.
She talked to me about my mother's anger,
the way women are and the mysteries
men and boys could never understand,
about her childhood in Escanaba,
her, not-unhappy, long, unmarried life,
and about Doug who appeared
from the adjoining room
at the Drake when she took me to Chicago.

Doug astounded me
while we sat one night by a campfire on the beach,
stabbing himself and laughing
while the jackknife quivered in his prosthetic thigh.
"He needs my care," she explained about
her empty bed in the room we shared.
"Doug's illness" accounted for the cries
and whispers through the wall.

Then slowly, there was less of Doug to love.
The following summer in Detroit
he dragged himself on crutches —
both legs deadwood now —
and the summer after that he was in a wheelchair —
his empty coat sleeve pinned to his lapel —
Then the summer we went nowhere,
and there was no Doug.

I never told my mother about Doug
when she quizzed me on my travels with Martha,
because Martha and I had our secrets,
because I didn't want to lose those summers,
and finally because
there was nothing more to tell.

A summer came when Martha didn't return,
another summer, and another two.

Then a small package arrived from Seattle
with a letter —
from Doug's little sister, it said —
an Inuit stone carving of a woman's face
emerging from the dorsal
of a dolphin with a chipped-off tail —
"Martha asked me to send you this,"
the letter said.
"She said you were someone she loved,
that was all, and that you'd love this little stone fish.
It keeps a secret, she said."

Each to Each

Dreaming, I wake up,
seeking my way between contradictions,
which, once reconciled,
leave no space to get through.

Mist sows its light
into all it obscures,
ten thousand circumambulations
of the sun —
every atom recycled, unceasing —

and if an infant body arrives,
bearing the spirit of Mozart
into our lives once again,
where else
would we think it could be?

Age

A dove cooing somewhere deep in the pine.

He kept hearing voices as he walked,
as if from high in the hills.

Yet when people spoke around him he felt
the edges fall away from their words.

He looked into the glare of the late August sun —
through the clustered needles —

through the dark silhouettes of heavy branches,
and couldn't find the sound of the dove.

Cloud Shadows

What we take with us
is our love for the things
we get past the Stygian *us*
at the gate —
as in an autumn weather,
wind growling through
the madrone,
cloud shadows sweeping the mountain
and the afternoon
as we watched them sail away.

Finally, This Rain

Every spring, foretold by its candles,
the pine grows that much taller.

Becoming the image of the image cast ahead
of what we hope to become —

stars continually revising themselves
and stars too faint to be named

translate the great dark hours of our being
into a language we love.

New Life

A tiny red spider,
not yet the size
of a pen point, skitters
back, and up, and
over the pale blue
grid lines on the notebook page,
fleeing the shock of its
sudden existence.

Aviatrix

Mayfly, Ephemeroptera,
delicate blue-winged-olive,
resting on my sleeve —
so happy to see you
in your glory again —
poised now for flight.

Will you know me
the next time we meet,
in whatever chrysalis
you may find me?

The Andromeda Galaxy

To see it, even as a faint green
swirl in the moonless dark, just

off the point of, and way beyond,
Alpha Cassiopeiae in the winter night,

is to see ourselves as best we can
with only slightly aided eyes,

as binoculars dip, and
rise, and there — tilted on its edge,

from where I stand, straining,
to see *us* as we might appear

if anywhere — in all the vast
splendor of its branching arms —

watching eyes and a curious mind
may have evolved their way

far enough through to look
in wonder at a smudge or swirl

in a great, dark space
beyond its local stars.

A Flea in Late Life

A flea, just landed on the large
Earth-globe in my study, has

for a full minute now — a month
or more in flea-time —

been crawling its way
north over western Canada, finally

entering the Arctic Circle and
steady on over the Beaufort Sea,

exactly to the Pole where it
pauses, rubbing its almost

imperceptible front legs together
as if conjuring a sign to show it

which of all possible Souths
to step into.

Neruda Falls

Rivers of the earth
often lose their names,

falling into a country
they pass through only once.

■ ■ ■

Neruda tells me there is water
falling through his head,

so fiercely he can't hear me he says,
yet waits, head cocked.

■ ■ ■

All around us, the absolute,
hiding in flowers and dung.

No, not *around us*, really.
The bees are busy in the lavender.

■ ■ ■

At any moment my pen may run out of ink
or my heart out of blood.

That bird is the butt-end of a broken branch
sticking up through the roadside grass.

■ ■ ■

I picked up a pinecone the size of a pineapple,
its spiny scales dripping with resin. Unwitting

kleptomaniac, now my fingers, eyes, heart, and tongue
cling to everything loved and fleeting.

■ ■ ■

Cows in the orchard, fireflies hiding light in the grass, a dove
explodes right under my feet, wing-beats whistle

like a rusty spring, as the last inundation of sky and sundown
wind settle in the cloak of the pines.

■ ■ ■

All my life I've been thirsty.
All my life I've craved salt.

Old Books

My life's companions, showing their age,
spines peeled back, bindings frayed, stacks

of brittle leaves, kept with tape and rubber bands,
though what they've said and have to say still

quickens the world behind my eyes,
and in a cloud that shadows me

with lightning, music, consolation—
sometimes peace and pure

delight in a darkness,
through which Sappho, Hui Neng,

or the night's soft wind brings
fuel to a lamp that flickers

and fades, flickers again,
and glows.

To Jim from the River

Jim Harrison 1937–2016

Still floating on the current,
this last stretch before the sea,

like so many we fished together
through what seemed an endless river

of summer afternoons — this one
as familiar as it isn't, hurrying more

the further we go — our conversations
about the words of which things are made,

stilled now to become just the things
themselves, the purling and the rings

of water reaching out from our casts,
heard now only with our eyes

as I stand in the bow, watching
my fly float high on its hackle

along the grassy bank,
careful not to let my gaze

drift back to where
you would always be,

sitting behind me, a wreath
of cigarette smoke —

the strange feeling you said
you sometimes had, letting

a trout go after all
the concentration of catching it —

more like Mozart
than Wagner, you said,

your good right eye
watching for the rise of a life,

your blind left, not too far
downstream, already absorbed

in that dark river light into which
we're constantly rowing.

Only This Morning

In a hundred trillion years —
an actual number
though we can't begin
to grasp it — the last traces
of our universe will be not
even a memory
with no memory to lament it.

The last dust of the last star
will not drift in the great nothing
out of which everything we love
or imagine eventually comes.

Yet every day, every four hours
around the clock, Debbie prepares
her goat's-milk mix
for the orphaned filly
who sucks down all three liters of it,
gratefully, it seems,
as if it matters more
than anything in the universe —
and it does — at this moment
while the sun is still
four hours from rising
on the only day that matters.

The Atom of the Actual

The poem is not *about*
anything but being, as it is,
a lens for our perception of
the occasion of its being.

A truth we can't visualize
but in the mind, manifest
by thought alone and know to be
no less real for being abstract —

Show us the truth, we said —
keeping in mind
the atom of the actual
we can't actually see — a different

sort of art to hold
with only thought for artifact —
not artificial, though contrived
by nature in the mind.

From a Ridge on Figueroa Mountain

And yet, as they say,
the heart is a leaf
and the wind makes it throb.

PABLO NERUDA

Down there somewhere, a breeze
is ruffling through a primrose bush,
and a tiny seed-spike —
       as if from a dandelion? —
is clinging to one of its leaves.

Why am I still roused by expectation
this late in my time
when everything that comes here
seems so easily lost?

I want to see where this new life goes,
whether it becomes a flower or a weed,
torn free now and alone,
which doesn't yet feel
quite like freedom.

Once Again, in August

I continue composing my love letter to Earth,
in all her beauty and affliction,
hoping I might love her
even a little bit more.

I write down the words
and blow on the paper
till the black ink stops shining
and the author is all but forgotten,

till the tree outside the window
is the live oak on the hillside,
and me,

till her leaves are the stars
of her own particular galaxy,
and mine,

till the blades of the grass surrounding her
are the evidence of her stubborn persistence,
and mine,

till the all-enveloping scrim of the sky
is her fragile blue cloak,
and mine,

till, in another five billion years,
she's blown into a cloud of hydrogen dust,
food for a future earth,
and I still haven't finished her song.

Brief Exquisite

The future happens every moment,
the way the shadow of a footfall
caresses the earth
an immeasurable breath ahead
of the foot.

Or so it seemed.

Index of Titles

Index of First Lines

About the Author

Dan Gerber is the author of eight previous volumes of poetry, most recently *Sailing through Cassiopeia* (Copper Canyon Press), as well as three novels, a collection of short stories, and two books of nonfiction. His honors include *ForeWord* magazine's Book of the Year Award in Poetry, the Society of Midland Authors Award, the Mark Twain Award, and the Michigan Author Award. His poems have appeared in *Poetry, The New Yorker, The Nation,* and *Best American Poetry.* He and his wife, Debbie, live with their beloved menagerie — domestic and wild — in the mountains of California's central coast.

Poetry is vital to language and living. Since 1972, Copper Canyon Press has published extraordinary poetry from around the world to engage the imaginations and intellects of readers, writers, booksellers, librarians, teachers, students, and donors.

WE ARE GRATEFUL FOR THE MAJOR SUPPORT PROVIDED BY:

THE PAUL G. ALLEN
FAMILY FOUNDATION

 amazon *literary*
partnership

 the POINT
envision·enact·evolve

 4
CULTURE

 golden
lasso

 Lannan

 ART WORKS. National
Endowment
for the Arts
arts.gov

 A&
OFFICE OF ARTS & CULTURE
SEATTLE

 SEATTLE
FOUNDATION

 WASHINGTON STATE
ARTS COMMISSION

TO LEARN MORE ABOUT UNDERWRITING
COPPER CANYON PRESS TITLES,
PLEASE CALL 360-385-4925 EXT. 103

WE ARE GRATEFUL FOR THE MAJOR SUPPORT PROVIDED BY:

Anonymous
Jill Baker and Jeffrey Bishop
Donna and Matt Bellew
John Branch
Diana Broze
Sarah and Tim Cavanaugh
Janet and Les Cox
Mimi Gardner Gates
Linda Gerrard and Walter Parsons
Gull Industries, Inc. on behalf of
    Ruth and William True
The Trust of Warren A. Gummow
Steven Myron Holl
Phil Kovacevich and Eric Wechsler
Lakeside Industries, Inc.
    on behalf of Jeanne Marie Lee
Maureen Lee and Mark Busto
Rhoady Lee and Alan Gartenhaus

Ellie Mathews and Carl Youngmann
    as The North Press
Anne O'Donnell and John Phillips
Petunia Charitable Fund and
    advisor Elizabeth Hebert
Suzie Rapp and Mark Hamilton
Joseph C. Roberts
Jill and Bill Ruckelshaus
Cynthia Lovelace Sears and
    Frank Buxton
Kim and Jeff Seely
Catherine Eaton Skinner and
    David Skinner
Dan Waggoner
Austin Walters
Barbara and Charles Wright
The dedicated interns and
    faithful volunteers of
    Copper Canyon Press

The Chinese character for poetry is made up of two parts: "word" and "temple." It also serves as pressmark for Copper Canyon Press.

This book is set in MVB Verdigris, a text face by Mark van Bronkhorst. Book design by VJB/Scribe. Printed on archival-quality paper.